Reconstruct Your Faith

Reconstruct Your Faith

Ancient Ways to Make Your Relationship with God Whole Again

Kevin M. Young, DMin

JOSSEY-BASS™
A Wiley Brand

Published simultaneously in Canada and the United Kingdom

ISBN: 9781394219490 (Hardback), 9781394219513 (ePDF), 9781394219506 (ePub)

Library of Congress Control Number: LCCN 2024007108 (print) | LCCN 2024007109 (ebook)

SKY10075033_051424

To my wife, Sally, who deserves it and believed in me, even when I did not,

and

to Libbie, Lucy, Harris, and Matthew, for all of the sacrifices that you have made.

Contents

Acknowledgments

It takes a village of expert herders to shepherd an author from proposal to publication. As such, I owe a debt of deep gratitude to the entire Wiley team, including Navin, Kezia, Pete, Sophie, and especially, Amy, who took a risk and believed in me. Also to Mark, Sarah, Jason, and Coal, whose feedback made this book far better.

To the staff and monks of the Abbey of the Genesee, thank you for your hospitality, homemade bread, and for rescuing my faith.

To Portland Seminary doctoral Cohort 13, where the roots of this journey began, as well as Loren, Cliff, Matt, Chris, Jordan, Nathan, and especially Leonard Sweet.

Acknowledgments

About the Author

Dr. Kevin M. Young is a pastor, speaker, consultant, coach, and avid weightlifter. He holds degrees in Media Communications and Theology from Cedarville University, Christian Education from Dallas Theological Seminary, and a Doctor of Ministry in Semiotics and Future Studies from Portland Seminary.

He is an award-winning producer in church communications and media production, and he has pastored several churches, one of which was named among the Fastest Growing Churches in America.

Kevin is Lead Clergy at Christ's Table, a hybrid ministry he founded to bring community, healing, and resources to those who are disillusioned, disconnected, or done with the institutional church but not God.

He is an NASM Elite Certified Personal Trainer and RP Nutrition Coach.

He is the cohost of the *Jacked Theology* podcast.

Kevin and his wife, Sally, live in Birmingham, Alabama, with their four children: Libbie, Lucy, Harris, and Matthew.

Introduction

> The room is almost all elephant. Almost none of it isn't.
> Pretty much solid elephant. So there's no room to
> talk about it.
>
> —Kay Ryan, "The Elephant in the Room"

Not one, but three.

That is the number of elephants in the pages of this book, and they are rather sizable at that.

Deconstruction is the first elephant in the room. The very word itself sends a cold shudder down the spine of the church. Depending on where you stand, deconstruction is either the greatest problem facing the church or it is the only hope for the church's future.

Passions run high on both sides. Lines have been drawn in the sand; churches are increasingly divided on the topic, as are families and friend groups. Entering a process of deconstruction of one's faith often sounds the death knell for all of a person's spiritual connections.

Deconstruction is almost always a desert experience.

Pastors are understandably concerned.

Be it harmful or healthy, deconstruction isn't just changing the nature of their congregants' spiritual journey, it is changing the landscape of the church itself. Many who deconstruct seem to walk away from the church, walk to a different church, or become advocates against certain dogmas in the church.

Deconstruction feels like an indictment, and that doesn't feel good at all.

If the word *deconstruction* is too harsh or off-putting a word, consider *disentangling*, *disassembling*, *deprogramming*, or *decolonizing* instead.

Try as the church might to prevent parishioners from traveling a path of deconstruction—or whatever we choose to call it—the church's attempts to control it have only fueled the fire, sending even more people down the path of deconstruction.

While most within the church would rather avoid the deconstruction conversation altogether, that may not be the best path.

Whenever there is an elephant in the room, we have options:

- Avoid it.
- Ignore it.
- Deny it.
- Silence it.
- Face it and hope to understand it.

Of those five options, "Face it and hope to understand it" is the preferred path, and within these pages that is the stance for which I will advocate.

Those who walk a path of deconstruction rarely desire to walk it alone. If they end up alone on the road, it is more likely that the church abandoned them than that they abandoned the church.

How do I know?

I am a fellow sojourner.

Reconstruction is the second elephant in the room. For those on the path of deconstruction, the word *reconstruction* can be quite off-putting. It brings a lot of baggage and assumptions with it, and those in the process of assessing their faith need unburdened hearts and minds.

I understand the concern. *Reconstruction* implies that:

- The process is as simple as putting the pieces back together again. *Usually, it's not that simple.*
- There is a single path to take on the journey. There isn't.
- A path must be taken at all. *That's false.*
- There will be an end to the journey. *There probably isn't.*
- One will never deconstruct again. *Cycles of deconstruction/ reconstruction are more likely.*
- It must be done as part of a church. *It doesn't.*
- One will remain within Christianity or still consider themself a follower of Christ at the end. *That isn't always the case.*
- Something must be done rather than nothing. *Some prefer to simply sit and be happy. Others prefer to sit and mourn.*

But in the end, we are bound to words, and while we may choose a different word—such as *remodel*, *reclaim*, *renovate*, *restore*, *renew*, or *reform*—we can hopefully all agree to allow others to make their own journey, or even no journey at all.

It is neither my choice nor yours as to whether a person reconstructs or the path they take to do it, if they so choose.

So why this book?

We all need an "alongsider," someone to walk with us on our journey. Though my path of deconstruction and reconstruction will differ from yours, it is helpful to know that you are not alone.

It is also easy to get overwhelmed, stalled, or stuck on journeys like this. It can be helpful, even hopeful, to know what helped others move forward. I also hope to convince you that you can and will make it through.

For those who desire to reconstruct a more Christ-like faith, I want you to see that it *can* be done. For those who aren't sure what they want, don't worry too much. I'm still not certain where my road leads either.

The third elephant in the room is me. Does the world really need another book by someone who looks like me? That is a valid question, if you are asking it. In many ways, I represent the church's greatest problem. I am a privileged insider.

I had an advantageous home situation (white, Midwest, middle-class, nuclear family), an advantageous educational journey (respected, conservative Christian universities and seminaries), and an advantageous career path (staff and senior pastor positions in some of the largest and fastest-growing churches in America).

But when a privileged insider begins using their voice to ask questions and question actions, the tides can turn quickly.

I am used to being an outsider to Evangelicalism, having grown up in the somewhat infamous Independent Fundamental Baptist (IFB) movement. We were King James Version (KJV) Bible-only, didn't go to movies, weren't allowed to dance or play cards, and were quite convinced of our own righteousness. While many of those who grow up in ultra-fundamentalism ultimately reject faith altogether, I did not. Instead of leaving, I bought a New International Version (NIV) Bible, became Southern Baptist, and went to see a movie.

In moments where many reject their faith, I pivoted. By the time I found myself in the throes of deconstruction, I had not only spent significant time in Baptist churches, but also seeker-sensitive, nondenominational, Evangelical Quaker, Calvary Chapel, and mainline congregations.

Over the years of ministry, I realized that I am hard-wired to be a *revolutionary*, one who fiercely and fearlessly advocates for needed change, challenging systems, ideas, and the status quo. But I am also hard-wired to be a *healer* and deeply driven to bring wholeness, health, and peace to brokenness.

Somewhere along the way, though, the church broke me.

This is the story of my deconstruction and how God is reconstructing me. This book is an invitation to join me on an ancient path.

PART I

Deconstructing Faith

1 How Did I Get Here?

> He who thinks that he is finished, is finished. Those who think that they have arrived, have lost their way.
>
> —Henri Nouwen

I can't believe I am here.

The thought had been rolling around in the recesses of my mind for days.

Perhaps, longer.

It was one of those uneasy feelings that a person gets deep in their gut when something, somewhere is off. The kind that begins as a simple nagging thought that gnaws at the edges of your sanity in moments of quiet reflection, but which, when unattended, becomes a raging fire of fear and self-doubt that threatens to overtake a person's spirit and irreparably wound their soul.

If I gave the worry my attention, I was wary of losing my soul. I was spiraling fast, and I was uncertain as to whether I had passed the point of rescue.

Was I too far gone to be rescued?

I can't believe I am here, I repeated to myself.

What was once just an abstract question about the direction of my life had become a very literal concern as I stood facing what was in front of me.

A set of doors.

Large ones. Very large.

These are the kind of doors that are designed to be imposing, to make one feel insignificant. The doors could not have known that there was no need to make me feel unwelcome or unworthy.

I had arrived broken, and, I feared, beyond repair.

On the other side of those doors lay hope … or confirmation of my defeat. We only arrive at these moments when we have no other options left.

Sometimes, the only way out of a storm is through it … through *those* doors.

Behind me, the gently rolling hills of western New York's Genesee Valley rose to meet the sun as the afternoon beams lit up the trees, setting their brilliant orange and yellow leaves afire on this late-Autumn day.

Beyond those hills was the life that I had all but outgrown. It was out there, behind me, awaiting my return. *But could I?* I had desperately tried to hold to the roots of my faith as the storm raged around me. I had desperately tried to avoid facing the difficult questions that threatened to destroy my faith. I had pushed everything down to the depths of the darkness within, hoping to forever avoid them. I was aware that questioning everything I thought I knew could destroy everything that I had ever built, or worse, dismantle everything on which I stood as a pastor.

Some questions are too dangerous to ask.

But the pain of going back to *what was* now seemed as unbearable as the thought of moving on, moving forward, into the unknown.

I couldn't go back, but I was too afraid to move forward. So I did the only thing that made sense as the storm raged around me … or more rightly, within me.

I planted my feet, firmly, resisting the strong urge to turn back or even look back.

I had come here for a reason. I had gotten to this place in my life for a reason.

I *had* to believe that.

I *had* to believe that there was some purpose in all that I endured, all that I had questioned, and all that I had lost.

The thought of Lot's wife crossed my mind, and for the first time, I felt compassion for this woman who grieved the loss of Gomorrah so much that she turned into a pillar of salt. Or, said less poetically, she cried herself to death in the crucible of deciding whether to return to a pain-filled past or move forward toward an even more uncertain future.

Here I was, at that same decision point.

Go back or move forward?

Not only was I standing in the way of moving forward, but so were the imposing doors of the storied Abbey of the Genesee, a place I hoped would be a peaceful eye in the midst of my raging storm. The Abbey is well known for bringing hope to those who have lost their way. Henri Nouwen, the venerable Dutch Catholic priest, professor, writer, and theologian, once stayed here, and it changed his life.

I hoped that it would change mine as well, but to be completely honest, there wasn't much hope left within me.

I was mostly numb.

So numb, in fact, that just moments earlier, I could barely look at the two-story cross I passed at the entrance of the Abbey. For reasons I could not yet fully face, I had bounced my eyes away from it.

I couldn't look at the cross, and the guilt I felt was profound.

It's just a cross, I told myself. *It's not like it's Jesus.*

But I had lost the ability to ignore the obvious disconnect between how these symbols once felt and how they felt now.

I was definitely numb.

Over the last few months, I had found myself avoiding nearly all of the religious rhythms that once brought me solace. There was no peace to be found in worship services, church community events, or even quiet moments of prayer. It is an odd thing for a pastor to find themself at odds with most of the primary expectations of their role. But my discontent had grown beyond my congregants and church. Religious symbols that once brought me peace, like the cross, now bore pain. Doctrines that had once brought assurance now brought unease.

My faith was in crisis.

I was in crisis. And I had nowhere to turn.

I avoided the cross at the Abbey because I was avoiding Jesus. It is as simple and as painful as that. I could no longer look Jesus in the eye, and that felt odd to admit. I preached about him on Sunday, but I avoided him on Monday. Better to avoid Jesus than have to face him with doubt in my heart, questions in my head, and growing concerns about everything I thought I knew about him.

So I skirted around the cross, not yet ready to confront it, hoping that in finding my way to the Abbey, I might find my way.

I can't believe I am here.

The massive doors of the Abbey—imposing and more than a bit ominous—looked down on me.

I felt small.

Unimportant in their shadow.

Both these doors *and* the cross seemed intent on reminding me of my insignificance.

I didn't need the reminder, to be honest.

The chaos that led to this storm had been brewing for years, I just hadn't seen it until it was far too late to be successfully avoided.

A faith that was once strong had been slowly dismantled from the foundation, brick by brick, over a long period of time.

I never expected the strength of my commitment to Jesus to be the very thing that unraveled my faith, yet here I was. It had been the *doing* of ministry that had led to my *undoing*.

And, I never saw it coming.

The Crumbling

Pastors aren't supposed to wrestle with faith. It makes congregations uncomfortable. We don't mind spiritual leaders asking hard questions of us, but we tend to prefer that they avoid asking hard questions about Christianity or the church. We want our leaders to have clear, bold answers, not questions.

I had questions.

I had a *lot* of questions.

I had questions about stuffy theological minutia that only even stuffier academics argue over, sure, but I also had a growing list of questions that gnawed at the edges of my mind.

- Was God's heart really set against the LGBTQ+ community?
- Were women second-class citizens in the Kingdom of God?
- Was racism really embedded in the U.S. church culture?
- Did the church really do more harm than good in the world?
- Was "telling the truth in love" really the way to show love?
- Were people who voted differently really in opposition to God?
- Was the Bible perfect and without error, and, if it was, how could we be certain that our interpretations were correct?
- Were we really loving our neighbor, or was that just something that we wanted to believe so we could assuage our fear and absolve our deeds?

I had questions, and these were just the tip of the iceberg. As a young boy in church, I learned that certain questions were okay to ask in church while others were better kept to oneself.

Good: "Is God a god of endless love?"
Not So Good: "Why did a loving God create Hell?

Good: "Does God love all people?"
Not So Good: "Am I welcome in the church if I am gay?"

Good: "Did God create everyone equal?"
Not So Good: "Can a woman be a Pastor?

Good: "Does God call us to care for those in need?"
Not So Good: "Can we let the homeless stay in our building?"
I had questions.

So I did what any respectable pastor would do with difficult questions—I shoved them down deep inside, first pretending they didn't exist, then hoping that more effective study and fervent prayer would sufficiently answer them. But every time I ignored them, they came clawing back, stronger than before.

I began to see how the church had oppressed, marginalized, minimized, and harmed the people it was supposed to protect.

My questions and deep concern began to spill out during sermons and Bible studies, during board meetings and back-hall conversations. I needed others to join me in the wrestling and wrangling of the ever-encroaching doubt, but, each time I shared a struggle, I saw fear in the eyes of the Christians I confided in and confessed to, not help.

- Should we really encourage others to vote for that person?
- Should we really exclude that person?
- Have we really thought about the ramifications of that doctrinal position and its scant support in Scripture?
- Have we really considered the other side of this issue and whether we are representing it fairly?

My questions were seen as a sign of weakness, not strength. It began to unravel my faith at the edges ... and, eventually, my ministry. I quickly learned that the only thing Christians like less than questions are questioners.

I was still as passionate as ever about following Jesus and leading others to him, but I was increasingly discontent with and within his church.

Religious fervor sometimes has a way of inoculating a person against reality.

The reality was simple: my faith was crumbling around me—my faith in the Bible, my faith in the church, and my faith in what I had been taught.

Only my faith in Jesus remained, and it seemed to be hanging only by a thread.

The Abbey was my Hail-Mary pass attempt. If I lost my faith in Jesus, I was certain that there was no salvaging any of the remnants of the faith that I once held so dear. But somewhere deep within, I was convinced that if I could reconnect to the roots—or the Root himself, Jesus—of my faith, then I could weather this storm, no matter the outcome.

Standing there at the Abbey, it felt like a hopeless attempt. The past few years had not only wrecked my faith, they had all but dashed my desire to ever be connected in any way to this thing called Christianity.

I no longer recognized the church, and I no longer saw much of Christ in Christianity. As I looked around, I wondered if the church would even be recognizable to Jesus, were he here. The questions kept me awake at night.

What would Jesus say to the Christians who blindly supported Donald Trump and those who followed his playbook? How would Jesus handle pastors who stoked the fires of Christian Nationalism? Would Jesus have applauded those who responded to the hurting members of the Black community with a curt,

"All Lives Matter"? How would Jesus respond to Christians who gave donations to build bigger border walls instead of longer dinner tables? Would Jesus have participated in the oppression of the LGBTQ+ community or been horrified by his followers who did? How would Jesus have responded to Christians who preferred gun proliferation over peace? Would Jesus have been shocked by the church's COVID response? How many tears would Jesus have shed over the sex abuse scandals in his churches and denominations?

The church's response to each of these had moved the needle in my heart just a bit. Each time, I wondered what it would mean to love my neighbors in the way that Jesus meant it when he said:

> *"You must love the Lord your God with all your heart, all your soul, all your mind, and all your strength." The second is equally important: "Love your neighbor as yourself." No other commandment is greater than these.* (Matthew 12:30–31)

Christians I had long respected took positions that caused very real harm to their neighbor. I saw a seemingly endless "ends-justify-the-means" mentality in Christian conversations, leveraging out-of-context scripture as justification for what amounted to hate, bigotry, and harm wrapped in "truth is love" rhetoric.

How could they not see it? I wondered.

Each issue took a toll on me, chipping away at my confidence that the Christians around me knew the meaning of "love your neighbor," let alone Christ. While I still deeply loved the church, I increasingly loathed its public witness. I have always loved the church, even and especially the broken ones. But here—at the doors of the Abbey, in the shadow of the cross—I had to admit that I never really wanted to be the pastor of any of them.

Why would any individual of sound mind knowingly subject themselves to the kind of pain and suffering that pastors endure?

Why would anyone want to be put on a pedestal that required them to project perfection?

Why would anyone commit to a career that required certainty in all things and allowed questions in no things?

The Power and Pain of Pastoring

I should never have become a pastor.

In fact, pastoring was never a part of the life plan. The rectory was never my trajectory. I had seen what bad churches do to good pastors, and I wanted nothing of it.

As I entered third grade, my stay-at-home mother re-entered the workforce as the pastor's secretary in our home church. I had no idea how much this move would affect my future, or my opinion of the church. I had special access to the pastors … and their pain. I saw the unseen problems they faced and the faces of the people who caused them.

I quickly learned that many Christians wear a costume on Sunday that they hang up on Monday, if they make it that long. It never made sense to me how some of the kindest, most seemingly Christ-centered people on Sunday could be the meanest on Monday.

And to this day, it still doesn't make sense. I hope that it never does.

Clearly, that hour on Sunday wasn't enough for some people, I thought.

Maybe that is why we also had Sunday evening *and* Wednesday Night worship services! But the people who had three times as much church seemed to be three times worse than those who didn't go at all.

Make it make sense! Why were so many Christians so very mean-spirited and intent on crushing others' souls while attempting to save them?

Everyone takes a gut-punch occasionally, sure, and sometimes friendly fire is unavoidable, even in the church. But years of seeing good pastors take punch after punch from people spewing hate speech out of one side of their mouth and Jesus speech from the other was too much. I wanted nothing of that life. I couldn't comprehend how a good person who tries to help others find God's love could be asked to endure an endless lack of love from people who professed God's love.

I love you, Jesus, but your church kind of sucks.

I was fairly certain that Jesus was aware and maybe even agreed with me. The Book of Acts confirms that Jesus left Earth just days before the first church was formed.

I wanted nothing of it.

Neither did my wife who is a P.K. (that is church-speak for "Pastor's Kid"). She had grown up seeing her father take friendly fire from a series of not-so-friendly churches. He eventually escaped from those congregations and planted a new kind of church focused on the unchurched; she barely escaped with her faith, vowing to never marry a minister.

Who could blame her?

Those who have experienced it understand: **church hurt is real.**

She didn't want to marry a pastor, and I very much wanted to avoid the pain of being one.

Perfect match!

We spent years serving the church together in various capacities, comfortably out of range of the worst arrows. We never imagined that we would end up being on the receiving end of church trauma or that we would be the target of hatred from fellow Christians simply for serving God.

But life sometimes has a way of wrecking our plans and sending us down paths we would have otherwise dared take. It was as if I was destined for the pain of pastoring. Try as I might to avoid it, I could not avoid church hurt because, simply put, I could not avoid the church. It was in my soul, embedded deep, and extracting it would have left too little of myself to have any real life thereafter. And when you truly love something, you will endure almost any pain imaginable to help heal it … not unlike Jesus did on the cross, a thought that continued to sit at the center of my mind during the intense trauma that would come.

The Painful Path to Disillusionment

I was 33 years old when I confessed to my wife that I was feeling a pull toward the pastorate. The age is seared in my memory as it is the same year that Jesus is said to have gone to the cross.

My growing discontent over the state of the church led to a sense of passion for pastoring. It felt wrong to clearly see the church's problems and then avoid any responsibility for fixing them. I realized that I had been running from God for three decades, and I had read the Book of Jonah, so I knew how that ended.

At 33, Jesus got the cross and I got a role as Senior Pastor. On the worst days, I wondered if crucifixion would have been less torture.

Churches are messy.

Church people are messier.

At first, everything was wonderful. It was a dream situation for a young pastor: a dying church in a decent suburb of a large metro area that already had everything necessary to be a thriving community of Christ followers … except hope. I knew from the get-go that this church was perfectly positioned to offer something different to the community.

Grace, not guilt.

Salve, not shame.

Healing, not hate.

Love, not legalism.

Nothing exceptional or radical, really. Simply Jesus. Just the things he taught in the red letters.

I had not accounted for the number of people in our community who just needed Jesus, nothing more. I was unaware of how many people had been burned by churches that promised one thing but delivered another.

The church began to thrive, not just numerically but spiritually. Everywhere I looked, new life was being breathed back into long-dead things. The joy was palpable, and the experience was nothing like what I had witnessed in church before.

Was this what pastoring was supposed to be like?

People were coming from everywhere. We soon outgrew our Worship Center, adding additional service times and eventually a second venue. Our Membership Class moved to the largest classroom in the building, and our Spiritual Growth Groups were multiplying faster than we could find leaders. The local newspaper published a front-page article on me, and we were listed as one of the fastest-growing churches in America by *Outreach* magazine.

It all caught me by surprise … as did the pushback.

Things began to change. Metrics stalled. Momentum tanked. Things that once thrived died. Everything began to fall apart, and try as I might to stop it, nothing seemed to work. Soon, I barely recognized the church, and it became difficult to tell whether I was keeping Hell from getting into the church or protecting the world from it getting out.

Like people, churches have a choice when it comes to change. A person can want to get healthy, but if they aren't willing to change their habits, they are unlikely to be successful.

The first few weeks of any new change are easy, but old habits die hard. Sometimes it is easier to remain the same than it is to go through the pain required by change. When it comes to physical fitness, the pain comes in the form of muscle aches and smaller dinner plates. When it comes to church health, the pain that prevents change is usually as simple as a loss of power. New people can upset the balance of power; diverse people bring divergent opinions.

Jesus was passionate about diversity, inclusion, and the end of oppression. He taught that the Kingdom of God would be upside down from the ones to which we are accustomed. In God's economy, those who are last would finally be first.

Teaching these topics brought in the oppressed, as well as those disappointed or done with the church, but it won little favor with those long-standing congregants who had the most to lose. When I began talking about racism and the ethnic implications of the Bible's "love your neighbor" passages, I received strong pushback. Advocating for more diversity in leadership was met with resistance. A push to be more welcoming to the LGBTQ+ community was a no-go, even though a core value was to "love all." Speaking positively about a Democrat from the pulpit drew a strong rebuke from a particularly exercised Elder.

"That isn't the way we do things around here," he said.

That statement became something of a recurring theme in that pastorate . . . and future ones. Years later, my therapist summed up the problem: "You're a revolutionary, Kevin." Which was information that I could have used about a decade and a half earlier than when she gave it.

Like the word *revolve*, a revolutionary turns things around. But revolutionaries also challenge the status quo and upset systems that people aren't fond of having upset. Revolutionaries can bring radical and necessary change, sure, but they also often die as martyrs in the process.

I didn't desire a revolution as much as I dreamed of a church that was open-handed with its resources, open-hearted with its love, and open-minded in its thinking. I longed for a church that was more passionate about Micah 6:8's call to "Do justice, love mercy, and walk humbly with God," than it was passionate about being doctrinally perfect, politically powerful, and antagonistic to culture.

From where I sat, my congregants were increasingly demanding doctrinal purity, alignment with radicalized political parties and their leaders, and lusting after power more than piety. And my church was not alone. All of Evangelicalism seemed to be on a similar path, a path increasingly divergent from my own.

The more time I spent in the trenches of church ministry, the more I was convinced that my faith journey was on a very different trajectory than that of those around me. The more I learned about God, the Christian faith, and the Bible, the less I was able to reconcile what I saw in the church with what I felt reflected the heart of God.

I realized that I had a choice to make.

I could pretend that the church wasn't deeply broken, or I could face the feelings of unease that were burning deep in my soul.

I could no longer look away, but …

Could I walk away?

The question crushed my soul as I stood at the doors of the Abbey, stalled.

Reflect

1. What question has you stumped, stalled, or just plain mad?
2. Have you ever faced a significant spiritual crisis? What was it grounded in? What did you do about it?
3. Is there a question that you can't ask?

4. Many say that during difficult seasons, their faith was tethered to something. Is yours, and if so, tethered to what?
5. Is there a symbol of faith that brings you the most joy or peace? What symbol brings you the most pain or confusion?
6. How did you get here? Share the story of your faith journey (or lack thereof) to this point.

2 The Church

The door handle is the handshake of the building.
—Juhani Pallasmaa, Finnish architect

There has to be a handle here somewhere.

The doors of the Abbey were as daunting as the enormous cross that I had avoided in order to get to them.

The cross is a simple but imposing symbol that acts as a boundary between the safety and solace of the Abbey grounds and the world beyond. Passing the cross feels as though one has left the one world to enter another, wholly other.

As I stood at its doors, I could feel the peace of the Abbey all around me, but I was not at peace. Far from it. I was an island of internal chaos in the midst of the absolutely maddeningly calm sea surrounding me.

The past few months—perhaps years, were I to be completely honest with myself—had given me ever-increasing anxiety about the church. Houses of worship had ceased to be places of peace, becoming conduits of doubt, pain, and an endless array of unanswered questions. I had long since lost my ability to push down the feelings, put on a happy face, and pretend as though everything was alright.

Were I not the pastor, it is uncertain whether I would have gone to church at all. But what is a pastor to do whenever their call to ministry and spiritual crises comes into conflict? If a parishioner steps away, a few may notice. If a pastor steps away, everyone notices. And worse, there is little hope of returning to pastoral ministry once one leaves. Memories run long, and pastors who question the status quo can leave the congregants who trusted them feeling betrayed.

If I outed my doubts, I was out of a job. But worse, I wasn't certain that I could find a way back to faith or the church if I left. I had seen how merciless Christians can be to those who struggle and walk away. They are shunned, marginalized, and ostracized. I knew that if I left the church, I was on my own … perhaps forever.

Was it possible to have a relationship with Christ without his church?

The questions crushed me, and rather than face them, I did what I had always done and pushed them aside, hoping they would stay out of the way just a moment longer.

So here I stood, about to enter this place that was supposed to bring me peace, and dare I hope, answers. Only one thing was standing in the way of whatever was to be: my fear … and these monstrously daunting old-world architecture doors, which weren't doing a blessed thing to ease my anxiety.

Where the heck is the handle?

I stood staring at the doors for what seemed like an eternity.

How can there be no handle?

I looked around to see if anyone was watching.

No, I was alone.

I looked to the right and left of the doors to see if there was a handicap-accessible button to press. Nothing.

I waved my hands in front of the doors, wondering if there was a motion sensor or camera. I must have looked insane; I certainly felt a bit insane.

Still nothing but silence.

I half wondered if I needed to wait until the last light of Durin's Day.[1]

I stifled a nervous laugh.

This is a bit too on the nose, I thought.

Just another in a long line of places professing to provide welcome to weary travelers and safety to wary wanderers, offering nothing to either in the end.

This was looking to be another in a long string of disappointments from religious institutions.

Had I come all this way for nothing?

I sat down, cross-legged in front of the door, put my head in my hands, and wept. Were anyone watching in that moment, it must have been quite the sight. The feelings of exclusion from this Abbey, a place of hope, too closely mirrored my feelings about the church.

I felt utterly abandoned, and it was overwhelming.

This disconnected feeling wasn't new, though. I had been struggling with it for quite a while. The promises made to me by the church didn't match up to my experiences in it . . . at all.

I had grown up hearing that God is love and that those who were "red, yellow, black, and white" were precious in God's

[1] In J.R.R. Tolkien's *The Lord of the Rings,* Durin's Day is the first day of the dwarves' New Year and the only day when the light will fall in just the right place to reveal the way to open a secret door.

sight.[2] I had been raised to believe that we were to care for the poor and those in need. I had been taught from an early age that God accepts us as we are and that nothing could stand in the way of that radical love.

This kind of selfless, self-sacrificing love was the foundation of Christianity, I had been told. And I bought into it. I had become convinced that Christians were to be the Good Samaritan of the story, not the robbers. I was certain that Christians were supposed to be the Prodigal Son's father, celebrating those on the margins without question or qualm. I had come to believe that when Jesus said "Love your neighbor," there was no limit to who was my neighbor and how far I needed to go to love them.

I grew up believing the things I was taught about Christian compassion, forgiveness, and my responsibility to help the harmed and oppressed. As an adult, I worked hard to live them out in every way that could.

This is the way of Christ, which also meant it was the only way for a Christian to live … or, so I was told.

I was shocked as an adult to discover a church that was largely unrecognizable when compared to the one I had been taught to expect as a child. Rather than a church that saw itself as the hands and feet of Jesus in this world, I discovered a church that largely failed to love like Jesus. I was dismayed to find congregations filled with people who disliked diversity, turned their backs on the poor, and created walls around God's love to keep out others. I couldn't reconcile the disconnect between *what was* and *what was supposed to be.*

---

[2]"Jesus Loves the Little Children" is a children's hymn written by Clarence Herbert Woolston. Did anyone consider that teaching Sunday School children to refer to different ethnicities by colors, like red or yellow, might not be the best practice? What were we thinking?

How could the church dismiss from the table the very people with whom Jesus regularly shared meals?

I no longer recognized the church, but I held out hope that the Abbey would somehow reconnect me to it. Looking up at the doors once again, I noticed rows of beautiful stained-glass windows. They must be magnificent from the inside, if only I could get there.

While their presence didn't surprise me, my reaction to them did. I felt sadness and regret for the church. For centuries, stained-glass windows have been used to tell the story of God to people who were unable to read it for themselves. For centuries, the church's most compelling stories were reflected in the windows that surrounded its worship spaces.

But today, the most compelling story the church is telling is one of exclusion, bigotry, hatred, and harm. Ask a non-Christian about the church's story and they are more likely to mention sex scandals and political alliances than they are compassion, Christ, or the cross.

The church has lost its way.

It has forgotten its story.

My eyes, now open to all of the harm that the church had done, could not look away from it. How could I serve another day in a system that was desperately (but, hopefully, not irreparably) broken? How could I serve another day in a system that had desperately (but, hopefully, not irreparably) broken me?

I prayed that on the other side of these doors, I could find hope. I desperately wanted to believe that things could be different, that the church could be different … that *I* could be different.

If there was hope for me, then there was hope for the church.

If I could reconnect with Christ, then so could the church.

There was a feeling in my gut that said, "To advance you must retreat. To move forward you must go back." For reasons

I couldn't quite explain, I needed to get closer to Christ, which meant I needed to get closer to the roots of the church.

I was convinced that, were I to go back in time far enough, I would eventually land upon an era when the church wasn't a complete and utter embarrassment.

But how far must I go?

Though my questions about the Bible were growing, I desperately wanted to trust that its hopeful tone about the early days of the church were honest, that they were pure. I desperately needed to believe that all hope was not lost.

The Early Church

In the Bible, there is a two-volume book written by a first-century doctor by the name of Luke. The Gospel of Luke is volume I; the Acts of the Apostles is volume II. Luke is working to compile eyewitness accounts of the life of Jesus and the Early Church to convince a Roman officer by the name of Theophilus to not leave his childhood faith behind. Luke says that he wants his reader to "be certain of the truth of everything you were taught."[3]

Theophilus is not Luke's only reader, though. Sitting outside of the Abbey, I found myself reading over Theophilus's shoulder, hoping to find something to cling to as well. I longed to have my childhood faith back and believe that there was reason for hope. I needed to believe that there was a time when the church didn't act so insufferable and irredeemably broken.

And there it was—late in the second chapter of Luke's second volume—a glimmer of hope. Almost as an aside, Luke gives a few words about the Early Church:

---

[3]Luke 1:4. *Unless otherwise indicated, all scripture quotations are taken from the Holy Bible, New Living Translation.*

All the believers devoted themselves to the apostles' teaching, and to fellowship, and to sharing in meals (including the Lord's Supper), and to prayer. A deep sense of awe came over them all, and the apostles performed many miraculous signs and wonders. And all the believers met together in one place and shared everything they had. They sold their property and possessions and shared the money with those in need. They worshiped together at the Temple each day, met in homes for the Lord's Supper, and shared their meals with great joy and generosity ....[4]

At first, Luke's words feel a bit like propaganda, an advertisement intent on convincing Theophilus, and us, of something that isn't quite true. Can we *really* believe that things were *this* good? *This* perfect? Luke's assessment feels so improbable that it feels false. It doesn't match my experience in the modern church. It feels so far-fetched that many commentators and commentaries just assume that Luke has lifted the verbiage from some older less-than-truthful summary about the Early Church. In other words, they call Luke a liar.

But I wasn't quite so sure.

I had never paid much attention to these verses over the years, probably because on first read they sound a great deal like most any basic, run-of-the-mill worship service that you or I have attended in any number of churches or denominations. But the more I dug into them, the more I realized that 2,000 years or so of assumptions had become attached to these words.

Many of my assumptions were wrong.

Shocking, I know.[5]

---

[4] Acts 2:42–46.

[5] Those who know me aren't shocked.

The Early Church looked quite different from anything that I had yet to experience … .

The Apostles' Teaching

When I read that the earliest Christians devoted themselves to the apostles' teaching, I immediately imagine preachers, pulpits, and the pounding of fists for effect as exceptionally strict doctrine is loudly and proudly proclaimed. But this couldn't be further from the truth. In fact, if we continue to read Luke's Acts of the Apostles, we are never given a description of what the apostles' teaching contained. Just because it is listed first does not necessarily mean it was first priority. If it were, one would assume that it would be specifically laid out for us.

Instead, what Acts seems to indicate is that the Early Church tended to focus on a radical kind of *living* that prioritized lifestyle and actions over and above perfect belief. In Acts, we see a greater emphasis on following the way of Jesus from the teachings in the Sermon on the Mount and the parables rather than stoic adherence to strict doctrinal structures.

And let's be uncomfortably honest here: the Early Church had no doctrinal structures.

Think about how wild that is!

The Early Church couldn't pull out a "Statement of Faith" from a filing cabinet or point a potential convert to the "What We Believe" section of its website. The church couldn't bring out the Bible—it didn't exist yet (and wouldn't for a few hundred years)—and Jesus wasn't around to set people straight. As far as we know, Jesus left absolutely nothing written behind.

As much as some might like to think so, the earliest Christians didn't seem to be concerned at all about finding ways to subjugate women, promote Young Earth Creationism, define marriage, or solidify their positional statement on any particular doctrinal fad that we obsess over.

They seemed to have one string on their guitar, one thing that they cared about: Jesus and his way. They even referred to themselves, not as "the Church," but as "The Way."

The apostles' teaching was solely focused on helping people better know the way of Jesus.[6]

Fellowship

I read the word *fellowship* and immediately imagine church potlucks, midweek dinners in the Fellowship Hall, and coffee conversations between old friends before heading to Sunday brunch. The difficulty with this is, the way that we think of *fellowship* doesn't quite match the word that Luke uses. Luke uses the Greek word *koinonia*, which isn't quite like our word *fellowship. Koinonia* comes closer to "active participation" than camaraderie, and it is more like "sharing concrete things in common" than sharing conversations. In that sense, fellowship is more an outcome of *koinonia* than the meaning of it.

When *koinonia* is based more in the concept of active participation than simple conversation, it becomes a strong statement about the power of complex community over and above mere conformity. Many of us have never experienced this kind of *koinonia* in the church.

The church tends to be more about *conformity* than a diverse (and therefore, often uncomfortable) *community*.

So often, the fellowship that I experienced in the church was less about *koinonia* and more about affinity, i.e. whether or not everyone liked each other and looked like each other. *Fellowship* tends to cultivate and celebrate uniformity, but *koinonia* places priority on a patchwork quilt of diverse individuals, sharing all things in common for the common good.

---

[6] See also Acts 5:42 and 1 Corinthians 2:1–2.

True *koinonia* is inclusive, not exclusive. It finds a way to welcome and involve all. It breaks down barriers built between itself and neighbors. It reflects the beauty of diversity by encouraging all to come and be a part.

I had spent a lot of time over the years encouraging people to be a part of the church, but each time that I did, new people never seemed to stay for very long or feel very welcome during their time with us. I was beginning to question whether the church understood how to be truly welcoming. Most churches seemed to be like mine, a *koinonia* catastrophe.

The Breaking of Bread

This one seems pretty straightforward, but it isn't. There is a tremendously heated argument among academics as to what was meant by "the breaking of bread."

Was it a meal?

Was it the Eucharist/Communion?

Was it both?

Some English translations mention a meal but then insert extra language like, "including the Lord's Supper," which wasn't in the original text.[7] Don't be too undone that a phrase was inserted that isn't there. I'm sure they had good reason. But maybe you, like me, were surprised to find that while the text *might* be alluding to the Lord's Supper, it never explicitly states it. That matters.

For the earliest Christians, worship time was mealtime. There was no difference between a worship service and a church potluck. They were the same thing, much to the dismay of those who avoid potlucks like the plague.

It would be centuries before pulpits and pews would invade the worship space, pushing all of the tables away save one, the Eucharist Table. I was shocked to find that most theologians and

[7] Acts 2:42 and Acts 2:46.

Bible commentaries give little thought to the Early Church's mealtime practices. While they spilled a great deal of ink over the apostles' teaching, fellowship, prayer, and even charity, few pondered the power of the breaking of bread at a meal.

Luke would be dismayed, I think, as he goes to great lengths to include meals in these few sentences, twice. It is almost as though Luke knew we were going to miss it. He doesn't repeat apostles' teaching, fellowship, or prayer, but he makes a point to remind us that the Early Church centered food (bread) as a part of their gatherings.

Once I saw this, I couldn't unsee it.

Luke talks about food everywhere, both in his Gospel and in the Acts of the Apostles. Most of the biblical stories of Jesus eating or sitting at a table with others can be found in—you guessed it—Luke!

Prayer

I thought I knew everything that there was to know about prayer. It seems so simple. First, close your eyes. Second, talk. Three, say "Amen." What more was there to know?

My problem was, no matter how hard I tried, I never felt very good at prayer. Prayer never seemed to make me feel the way that I was told it should. During prayer, I rarely felt deeply connected to much of anything beyond my own needs. Like most people, my prayer life consisted of little more than an ever-growing list of requests that I would pass off to God, with my head bowed and eyes closed.

But I was in for a bit of a shock. The original Greek text doesn't say that Early Church believers devoted themselves to prayer; it says something slightly different. Literally, the Early Church believers devoted themselves "to *the* prayers."[8]

---

[8]Acts 2:42. Many English translations delete the word "the" from the text.

The word *the* stopped me. *The* prayers, it says, as though there were specific prayers. If that were the case, it would change everything that I thought I knew about prayer.

I had been raised to believe that prewritten prayers prayed out of routine or obligation didn't count as much as those made up on the spot. Prayers from the heart were better, I was taught. But here, there is a hint that I may have been wrong.

The Early Church seems to have prayed specific prayers.

Sharing Resources

Here, I must begin with a confession.

During my early years as a pastor, I only ever taught the first four things on the list: the apostles' teaching, fellowship, the breaking of bread, and prayer. I even had a catchy name for the series of sermons, "The Fantastic Four," a name which conveniently avoided the fifth area to which the Early Church is said to have devoted themselves.

Giving.

Ugh.

Can I be honest about giving and sharing? I'm not a huge fan of it. And if you were being completely honest, you probably aren't either. Yes, we may not mind giving to people who we love or feel are deserving, but how about those who we don't love or who aren't so deserving?

Luke pulls no punches in Acts as he flatly states that the Early Church practiced a kind of radical giving that would even make a modern socialist flinch. Luke points out that the earliest Christians held everything in common, even and especially their possessions. They even sold their property *and* gave the proceeds to anyone in need. But while Luke is explicit on the importance and power of this point, many theologians and pastors side-step this fifth ingredient altogether. It is often ignored.

Giving until it hurts, hurts, I guess.

If your pastor ever danced around the giving practices of the Early Church, or ignored them, it may be because most Bible commentaries do as well. Most commentaries downplay the need rather than simply admit that we tend to fail miserably at following them. Some commentators point out the "imperfect tense" of the Greek, suggesting that *sharing* was a suggestion but was never enforced. A few admit that the Early Church did sell property to fund charity, but they caution that the disposal of private property was not a once-for-all command. They suggest that it is more rightly seen as a preference of the Early Church but not a mandate.

As I read them, One by one, each commentary cautioned, critiqued, or outright criticized the radical giving practices of the Early Church, one going so far as to suggest it amounted to communism (which in their mind, was obviously ungodly). Each sought to limit the implications of the Early Church's practice in one way or another.

A boundary here. A border there. All vacating—in all or part—the power of a lifestyle that isn't possessive of one's possessions.

Oddly enough, I couldn't find a pastor, theologian, or commentary that tried to limit the practice of the first four items. There was no nuancing the Greek to suggest that we be cautious of praying too much. Not a single commentary suggested that a Christian should be careful to avoid following the apostles' teaching too closely. And certainly no one suggested that anyone eat less.

I couldn't help but feel as though those intent on teaching the texts to me were equally intent on avoiding the more difficult aspects of The Way of Jesus.

I wondered how many other times those I trusted to train me had used logical and theological gymnastics to avoid allowing the Early Church's actions to carry its full force? I wondered how many times I had ignored the example set by the earliest Christians?

I looked up at the Abbey again, wondering what else I had missed.

Hoping.

Longing.

Desperation.

I *needed* to believe that there was hope beyond what I could currently see in the church and here at these doors.

Finding a small measure of resolve, I stood up and placed my hands on the doors of the Abbey, almost as a prayer.

I needed to *do* something.

I needed to *feel* something.

And I did.

I felt it.

Hope.

… and a handle!

It had been there all along, hiding in plain sight. Both the handle and the hope.

We often pray for the dramatic, mountain-moving moments where God's presence is unquestionably on display … at least, if you are like me, you do.

We want to experience the clarity of the burning bush, the presence of the fourth man in the fire, and the power in the parting of the Red Sea. We long for the supernatural display that calms our questioning soul and sends courage coursing through our spiritual veins.

But God rarely chooses to move in such ways.

There is a line from one of the songs in the Book of Psalms that has long haunted me. In it, the songwriter reveals something important about the voice of God:

> "Your word is a lamp to guide my feet and a light for my path.[9]"

Rather than shock and awe, God seems to prefer the small and personal. His guidance for us, says the Psalmist, is less like sunlight and more like candlelight. Yes, God will give us light for our journey, but following him may often be more like stumbling around in the darkness than running in the noon-time sunlight.

We all like to see the full path ahead of us, but running at that speed can create nasty bruises when we get tripped up and fall. God seems to prefer a different pace.

Just enough light to see what's next and trust the rest.

Just enough light to see the handle when I need it.

Just enough sight to see the next step when I'm ready to take it.

It was time. Time to leave behind the whirlwind and face whatever was next, come what may.

I grasped the handle firmly and pulled on the door with all the strength I could muster. It was time to take the first step into the unknown.

The only way out was forward.

---

[9] Psalm 119:105.

Reflect

1. Has your experience with the church been positive or negative?
2. What promises has the church made that you feel were false or that failed?
3. Which of the five items that Luke lists—apostles' teaching, breaking of bread, fellowship, prayer, sharing resources—are you most drawn to? Which are you least drawn to?
4. Is there any area in which you feel the dim light of Christ?
5. Is there one small step that you can take at this moment?

3 The Bible

> No man ever believes that the Bible means what it says: He is always convinced that it says what he means.
>
> —George Barnard Shaw

The Abbey of the Genesee is home to several dozen Trappist monks. The Trappists are famous for following some of the oldest rules of order practiced by Christian monks, and especially, for taking a lifetime vow of silence. These monks have given the rest of their lives to prayer and reflection. In order to accomplish that, they strive for silence, speaking only when necessary as they go about their daily tasks in the Abbey's enclosure.

The monks aspire to become the living embodiment of prayer without ceasing.[1] Unimportant conversations interrupt contemplative prayer, so the monks spend their day avoiding

[1] Based on 1 Thessalonians 5:17.

small talk so as to center on prayer. If something doesn't absolutely need to be said, they don't say it.

It was that very thing that had drawn me to this particular Abbey. I needed to sever myself from the competing voices in my life, especially the voices of pain that were encroaching upon my heart like an insidious cancer.

I desperately hoped to drown out the others in silence and hear God's voice again, a voice that had been maddeningly silent during my extended dark night of the soul.

What I had very much not expected on this silent retreat at the Abbey was five hours of worship—speaking, chanting, and singing—spread throughout the day and night, led by the monks. The monks' vow of silence did not extend to the Sanctuary of the Abbey. Here, they could use their voices in prayer and song. And pray they did!

I select a seat at the end of the pew closest to the Abbey doors—which also happens to be the closest to the exit, just in case I have an anxiety attack. The pew is empty, save for me. It will remain empty for the rest of the hour of prayer, as would the rest of the pews before and behind me.

Even here in this holy place—among other men of the cloth—I am painfully and desperately alone.

The sizable seating area is separated from the monks by a waist-high barrier. It creates an *us* and *them* feeling, dividing the

Abbey into sacred space and what I come to think of as *my* space. I'm not on holy ground, but I can see it from here.

Each pew seat has its own songbook, an unnecessarily large—four times the size of a hymnal—ornate Book of Psalms that is hand-lettered in Old-English calligraphy. Beautiful, but difficult to read.

The Psalms are their songbook, and next to it is a heavily worn sheet of paper listing the psalm-songs for each service of the week. While it is obvious that the monks are chanting from somewhere within the songbook, their chants do not match the song list on my sheet.

I am immediately and hopelessly lost.

My heart sinks as I experience the profound confusion and subsequent frustration that comes from sitting in a religious worship service where everyone expects you to understand what is happening, but you don't.

Allowing my mind to wonder, I begin to take in the grandeur of this space. It is breathtaking. The cathedral ceiling towers above the sanctuary space, held in place by concrete buttresses and steel girders that cross above my head. Rows of stained-glass windows allow the failing light of day to fall across the floor, spilling their dance of color on everything they touch. Between the ceiling and floor, the walls of the sanctuary are built of river rock, large boulders grounding the space in a way that also serves to ground me to something deeper. Even in the midst of my internal storm, I am struck by the soaring peace of this place.

If God is to meet me anywhere, surely it will be here.

Dear God, let it be here, I thought.

If I didn't walk out of here with a renewed faith, I was fairly certain that I would end up walking away from it all for good … or, at least, for my good.

Intent on avoiding the *what ifs,* I look around again, searching for something to distract me from the feeling of helplessness that is quickly encroaching on this small oasis of peace. And there it is; how could I have missed it? On an almost-out-of-sight board there is a list of last-minute changes to the psalter schedule.

The usual psalms for this service have been replaced with Psalms 141 and 142:

I cry out to the Lord;
I plead for the Lord's mercy.
I pour out my complaints before him
and tell him all my troubles.
When I am overwhelmed,
you alone know the way I should turn.
Wherever I go,
my enemies have set traps for me.
I look for someone to come and help me,
but no one gives me a passing thought!
No one will help me;
no one cares a bit what happens to me.
Then I pray to you, O Lord.
I say, "You are my place of refuge.
You are all I really want in life.
Hear my cry,
for I am very low.
Rescue me from my persecutors,
for they are too strong for me.
Bring me out of prison. …"[2]

[2] Psalm 142:1–7a.

I sat in stunned silence.

The words of the psalm wrapped their fingers around my soul and squeezed, sending tears streaming down my face. Some deep well within me had been plunged, and the power of the waters that flowed from it caught me off guard.

God?! Are you here?

I couldn't remember the last time I had sensed God's voice in the texts of the Bible. The shock of feeling God's presence in the words of this surprise psalter was nearly as disconcerting as the realization, years ago, that I no longer sensed God's presence in the Bible itself.

... at least, not like I once had.

The Bible Is Not God

Everything seemed so simple in my younger years.

The Bible was God's inspired, infallible, and inerrant word, and the greatest of these was inerrancy. The Bible was presumed to be without error, and its perfection was never to be in question. We were taught to elevate the Bible above all else ... and fear it.

"God said it. I believe it. That settles it."

This phrase about the Bible was beaten into my head by the pastors and teachers under which I first found faith. It amounts to Bumper Sticker Theology—the kind that fits nicely on a billboard but also packs a punch when delivered—and there was a lot of Bumper Sticker Theology within Evangelicalism.

Evangelical theology was meant to punch hard and leave a mark. The trick was to come away from it without too many bruises.

I came to see that the Bible was not only used to guide belief, but was often used to bully people into belief or back into compliance if a person's beliefs drifted too close to the margins. If someone was drinking bourbon or beer, we would point to a verse and say, "See, right there. Stop that." Or if a well-meaning person openly questioned a firmly held doctrine—no matter how inconsequential it might be—we would pull out a large Reference Bible, point to a verse or two about submission, and push them back in line.

For us, the Bible was the final arbiter of literally everything. It was the judge, jury, and executioner.

It was that "executioner" part that finally began to break apart my biblical theology. There are only so many friends that a person can watch walk out of the revolving back door of the church before one begins to ask some questions and do some introspection. There comes a point when we must admit that lines like, "They never believed to begin with," or "They wanted to go sin rather than sit under sound teaching," just don't fit the character of the people who walk away. There is a point at which we must pay attention to those who threw up their hands in desperation over our treatment of the Word of God.

Even that phrase itself, the "Word of God," was a large part of the eventual dismantling of the beliefs I had built the foundation of my faith upon. I had been taught to misunderstand it.

When the Apostle John makes a reference to "the Word" at the beginning of his Gospel, it is important:

In the beginning the Word already existed.
The Word was with God,
and the Word was God.
He existed in the beginning with God.
God created everything through him,
and nothing was created except through him.
The Word gave life to everything that was created,
and his life brought light to everyone.

The light shines in the darkness,
and the darkness can never extinguish it.[3]

It *is* important, but we also tend to misunderstand it.

For a long time, I assumed that the word *Word* in John 1 was an allusion to the Bible. Preachers of my youth probably had more than a little to do with this, as rarely a week went by before they would recite these opening words of John's Gospel while waving a large, threadbare KJV in the air. "The Word" became synonymous with "the Bible."

It was as though the text read: *In the beginning* ***the Bible*** *already existed.* ***The Bible*** *was with God, and* ***the Bible*** *was God.*

The problem with this kind of thinking—other than being blatantly false—is that it makes the Bible an idol. And the Bible itself tends to take a very dim view of idolatry ... even idolatry of its own writings. God tends to not take kindly to sharing the throne with anyone or anything (which is what idolatry essentially is: replacement of God with something that is not God).

The Bible *is not* God.

The Bible *is not* equal with God.

The Bible *is not* worthy of worship.

It's understandable that we would have difficulty avoiding mishandling texts like John 1 and end up declaring the Bible the de facto "Word of God." The word *Word* in John 1 is notoriously difficult to translate, and it may well be the most difficult word to translate in the New Testament, if translatable at all. Many scholars throw their hands up in the air and don't try to translate it.

But let's throw caution to the wind and try! My home church pastor with his Scofield Reference Bible likely already

[3] John 1:1–5.

considers me a heretic by this point anyway, so what do we have to lose?[4]

Most English translations use the longstanding and traditional word *Word* to represent the Greek word *Logos*. But *Word* is a rather terrible, inadequate, and even misleading translation of *Logos* because it implies *words*. And written or spoken *words* are exactly NOT what the word *Logos* intends to imply.

So what does *Logos* mean?

Our English translations give us a hint by capitalizing the word *Word*. John goes a bit further to help when he says that "the Word (Logos) became human and made his home among us."[5]

The rest of the chapter goes on to make clear that Jesus is the *Logos*, the Word of God.

The "Word of God" is Jesus, not the Bible.

Jesus Is the Word

Troy Martin, Professor of Religious Studies at St. Xavier University, gives the best translation of *Logos* that I've ever run across. He suggests that the best understanding of *Logos* is offered by DNA. Through Jesus, says Martin, we are able to experience the living and enduring DNA of a living and enduring God.[6]

What I love about the idea of the *Logos*—i.e., Jesus—being best represented in the Gospel of John as DNA is that DNA

---

[4] Published in 1909, it would be impossible to overstate the importance of the Scofield Reference Bible to the 20th-century Fundamentalism and Dispensationalism movements, within which I grew up. I was raised in an Independent Fundamental Baptist (IFB) Church, and for us, the Scofield Reference Bible was closer to the heart of God than the tablets he handwrote to Moses on Sinai.

[5] John 1:14.

[6] Troy W. Martin, Translating Logos as DNA in First Peter 1:22–25, https://doi.org/10.2307/j.ctv138wrtq.11.

carries all of the genetic instructions required for development, function, growth, and reproduction within living creatures.

Jesus, then, is the stuff of life.

Jesus is what is necessary for the development, function, growth, and reproduction of faith, not the Bible.

It shouldn't be a surprise that John chose to start his gospel with a dissertation on Jesus being the universal catalyst for the development, function, growth, and development of life. John makes his view of Jesus crystal-clear a little later when he quotes Jesus as saying, "My purpose is to give [people] a rich and satisfying life."[7]

Life.

Full. Satisfying. Life.

What even is that? . . . Life?

As I looked around the Abbey, I realized that I desperately wanted to feel life. I wanted to feel alive. I wanted to feel … something.

For so long, all I felt was numb.

I breathed in deeply and exhaled, allowing myself to settle into a rhythmic breathing pattern that had often brought me peace in the moments where anxiety began to creep up from within.

Breathe, Kevin. Breathe.

We've got this.

I listened to the sound of the breath as I made it.

"YH" … breathe in.

"WH" … breathe out.

The ancient Hebrews' personal name for God is more of a breath than a formed word: *YHWH.*

"YH" … inhale.

"WH" … exhale.

---

[7]John 10:10b.

The very name of God is formed not by words on lips as much as air through breaths.

"YH" … inspire.

"WH" … expire.

The breath of life, on our lips. God's name, breathed in rhythmic time to the inhale and exhale of life. God, wrapped up in the inspiring and expiring of the breath of life.

I pondered the thought of God having always been in my lungs. I sat with the realization that even when I couldn't hear God's voice, if I listened closely enough, I could feel God's presence through the inspiration of oxygen into my body.

As my faith in the church faltered, I realized that the inspiration of God through the simple rhythm of breathing had kept my faith in Jesus alive. My faith was on life support, perhaps, but alive.

YHWH.

It's really not so radical a thought. The Bible itself even seems to confirm it throughout its pages. When we can't hear God, God is still there in the breath that sustains and maintains us.

We see it at the very beginning, for instance, whenever God animates Adam. His tool of choice? Breath.

> … *God formed the man from the dust of the ground. He breathed the breath of life into the man's nostrils, and the man became a living person..*[8]

God's breath inspires Adam, giving him life. Or said differently, God's breath makes Adam fully alive. Adam is made alive through divine inspiration.

But this isn't the only place we see this phenomenon.

---

[8] Genesis 2:7.

A bit later, in the story of Moses, there is an argument between Moses and his brother Aaron and his sister Miriam. As Moses' siblings step up to oppose Moses as the primary conduit of God's words and message, God steps in to defend Moses, saying:

I speak to him face to face, clearly, and not in riddles! He sees the Lord as he is.[9]

If we were to dig into the language used here, though, "face to face" isn't the closest or best translation of the actual words used by God. And it is understandable that the translators would flinch because the literal text is more than a little awkward. Perhaps the translation team attended a "True Love Waits" event as teens growing up inside Evangelical purity culture and were concerned that this spicy scene between God and Moses would ignite too much passion and too many questions.

Rather than "face to face," God is said to speak to Moses "mouth to mouth."

Breath intertwined.

Intimate.

This isn't just closeness, this is deep intimacy.

Intimacy, therefore, is the point of inspiration.

God's breath, intimately entangled with everything inside of us, giving life. God was mouth to mouth with Adam at creation, now here again with Moses, and also with us.

If you have ever tried it, there is an interesting thing that happens whenever you are mouth to mouth with someone—be it locked in a passionate kiss or a less than sensual CPR event—words are impossible to speak. You can't be mouth to mouth and form words.

Inspiration isn't words.

---

[9]Numbers 12:8a.

So when the author of 2 Timothy makes the rather famous statement that "All Scripture is inspired by God and is useful ...,"[10] we often get its meaning wrong. If we think that *inspiration* means "God-breathed," then we are getting close. But if we think of words on the page, then we are moving away from the meaning.

Inspiration means that the words of God, how they come to us, are "life-giving" in a way that is only possible by being mouth to mouth with the source.

As I sat in the Abbey, struggling to hear God's voice and find mine, it dawned on me that there are only two things in history that are said to be inspired. Only two things are ever mentioned to be breathed into by the breath of God:

- Human beings
- Scripture

It began to become clear to me in that peaceful place that we have been misusing the Bible in order to abuse. For so many years, *I* had been misusing the Bible.

The Bible was supposed to give life, not take it. The texts of Scripture were supposed to breathe life, not destroy it. The Bible

[10] 2 Timothy 3:16.

was supposed to be mouth-to-mouth resuscitation for those moments when our spirit is dying.

The Bible was intended to revive people like me in moments like this; it was meant to be CPR for a dry and weary soul.

I gathered my emotions and tried as best I could to plug back into the prayer service. I couldn't help but feel as though something from the song text from Psalms had resuscitated something deep within me.

Is it possible that God still speaks ... and speaks to me?

A monk made his way to the lectern, a rather unimposing piece of furniture off to the side of the sanctuary. I grew up seeing pulpits designed to command the room and sitting in the center of everything, but this one seemed to be intentionally unassuming.

The monk opened the Bible to read the assigned text for the evening. "The Word of the Lord," he began, "from the Second Letter to Timothy ...."

In that moment, my soul settled just a bit. The monk could not possibly have known that this particular letter attributed to the Apostle Paul—written to a young, struggling pastor like me—had long been a favorite. He could not have known that, but there was One who did.

Do I still believe that God speaks?

And as though I was hearing from a voice from whom I had neither heard nor felt in far too long:

> *... Chapter Four:*
>
> *I have fought the good fight, I have finished the race, and I have remained faithful. And now the prize awaits me—the crown of righteousness, which the Lord, the righteous Judge, will give me on the day of his return.*[11]

---

[11] 2 Timothy 2:7–8.

In that hour of prayer, somehow, the breath of God had blown away a bit of the ever-encroaching doubt in my soul, leaving in its place a single flickering flame of hope.

It seemed so weak, but it was hope.

I dared not yet believe that I was to be rescued from my dark night of the soul, but also, I was now unable to unequivocally state that God had forgotten me and left me in my struggle and pain.

As I made my way out of the Abbey and into the darkness that had fallen, I felt just a bit more light within my heart than when I had first entered. The door of the Abbey even seemed a bit less imposing than it had when I had first arrived.

Had it changed, or had I?

One thing that had definitely changed was my relationship with the Bible. Our status had been updated to: "It's complicated," and that felt like real progress.

Reflect

1. Is the thought of the Bible a positive or negative one for you?
2. If the Bible is not the judge, jury, or executioner, what role can it play in your life?
3. What would a "full life" for you look like?
4. Have the words of the Bible breathed life or destruction into your life?

4 Inerrancy

> O Lord, bless this thy hand grenade, that with it thou mayst blow thine enemies to tiny bits, in thy mercy.
>
> —Cleric, *Monty Python and the Holy Grail*

Exiting the Abbey brought down a blanket of darkness upon me again.

Night had fallen.

I was used to this feeling, ominous … yet somehow, no longer so overwhelming.

The cross that had seemed so imposing upon entering the Abbey seemed less so now, and oddly, within its brilliantly lit crossbeams I felt a twinge of peace.

A twinge.

As a symbol, the cross has long been used to bring both peace and pain. For 2,000 years it has brought some closer to Christ but pushed others farther away.

It is difficult to rescue and redeem a symbol from those who are intent on abusing it.

I just could not get past the cross, in both a literal and figurative way.

Though my emotions were raw, and the flicker of hope in my soul was tenuous, I was still drawn to it. The cross, the symbol that I had avoided in my darkest hours, did not yet bring hope, but there was now something about this symbol that captured my attention.

I had been taught to see the cross through the lens of fear and suffering, pain and punishment.

Had I been taught wrong?

The path from the Abbey to the cross may have been easily navigated under the light of day, but darkness brought more than a little difficulty as I tried to traverse the rough path. Though the cross was illuminated by several high-powered spotlights, there was barely enough light to navigate the path through the darkness. Each step required a measure of clarity and a bit of courage, so as not to stumble.

I couldn't help but laugh at the literal words of Psalm 119:105 being true in this moment, God's Word (Jesus) being a lamp to my feet and a light to my path, leading me back to him … or, at least, to this symbol of him set as a beacon of brilliant hope in the midst of the darkness that surrounded the Abbey.

It would be difficult to over-sell the size of this cross. It was enormous. The base of the cross was set into a large, circular concrete slab surrounded by stone. Stepping up to the stone, I stood for what felt like an eternity. Staring up at the cross, I was lost in an emotional chasm of knowing and unknowing.

I knew so much about Jesus, the cross, and the salvation it is said to offer. But I also had the overwhelming feeling that I still knew far too little about the mysteries of the cross and Christ.

Without thinking, my lips began to mouth, then sing, the words to a song that had been beaten into my head during countless altar calls as a child: "I Surrender All." As a teenager, I had come to hate this song. We sang it so often that I began protesting its inclusion by refusing to sing it.

But here I was now, singing it, as though it were the last handle I had to my faith. Perhaps it was.

It is weird how the things that are so seemingly insignificant at the time, like a simple song, end up becoming the deep bedrock upon which the last vestiges of one's faith cling during the storms that threaten to destroy it.

All to Jesus, I surrender,
All to Him, I freely give,
I will ever love and trust Him,
In his presence daily live.[1]

I dropped my eyes to the ground, unable to look at the cross any longer, my heart racked with a flood of feelings. Each of them, crashing over me like waves, the next greater than the last.

Guilt.

Hope.

Shame.

Desire.

Repentance.

---

[1]Judson W. Van DeVenter, "I Surrender All," public domain.

Love.

Anger.

Peace.

Frustration.

Every emotion that had been pushed down—years of feelings and fears—came rushing out all at once … all of them, all at once, channeled toward the cross.

"I have tried!" I shouted.

Dear God, I have tried to surrender all.

I realized in that moment that my problem wasn't Jesus.

I dropped to my knees, not so much out of reverence, but out of an overwhelming feeling of being unable to carry the load that I had been carry any longer.

All to Jesus, I surrender,
Humbly at his feet I bow.

The cold, unforgiving slab of concrete reminded my heart … and my knees … that sometimes, humble bowing can be a bit uncomfortable. Repositioning, I noticed that the concrete causing me discomfort was the same concrete that held the cross in place, unmoved. For better or for worse, the cross would always be here, unmoved, thanks to the concrete. No matter the storms that raged around it, no matter the strength of the wind or the force of anyone who might try to come along and move it, the Abbey cross would remain strongly grounded in the concrete into which it had long been set.

My faith had long yearned for something to cling to, something impervious to outside forces, feelings, and fears.

My faith longed for concrete.

For years, *this* cross had done just that: weathered storms.

For years, *the* cross had done that as well.

Maybe the problem wasn't in my faith, but in my thinking.

I had given my heart to Jesus, but I'd been taught to trust the Bible. Somewhere along the way, Christianity had decided that Jesus was the gateway to the Bible, and after one became a follower of Jesus, you were handed off to the Bible to take it from there … "Thank you, Jesus. We've got it from here."

"Just trust the Bible," we were told. "Check back in with Jesus on Christmas and Easter if you need anything, but otherwise, you've got the Bible to get you through. And for heaven's sake, don't question it, argue with it, or dismiss anything that it says as being anything less than perfect."

My problem wasn't Jesus or the cross, it was the Bible.

Transparently, I wasn't sure that I could stomach the Bible anymore.

The Bible was standing in the way of Jesus, and I'm not certain how it got there. It definitely wasn't Jesus' doing. He had made his stance on the matter absolutely clear in his final words to us in what we sometimes refer to as the Great Commission:

> *Jesus came and told his disciples, "I have been given all authority in heaven and on earth. Therefore, go and make disciples of all the nations, baptizing them in the name of the Father and the Son and the Holy Spirit. Teach these new disciples to obey all the commands I have given you. …"*[2]

I can remember pastors teaching this text from huge wooden pulpits with an enormous cross on the front. The preacher would get to that line, "Teach these new disciples to obey all the commands I have given you … " and pause for dramatic effect. Sometimes they would pull out their handkerchief and wipe their brow. That was how we could tell that something really important was coming. A smile would slip across their face, and

---

[2] Matthew 28:18–20a.

the preacher would pick up the impossibly huge Bible they were using, hold it out in front of the pulpit, and shout: "Teach these new disciples to OBEY ALL THE COMMANDS I have given you!"

Then the preacher would again pause for dramatic effect. We all knew what he was waiting for. If only a few people in the audience shouted an "Amen!" in response, the preacher would hold the Bible a bit higher and bellow even more loudly, **"TEACH THESE NEW DISCIPLES TO OBEY ALL THE COMMANDS!"**

This might go back and forth a few times until everyone was whipped into a frenzy. We, of course, all knew what he meant. Whenever a preacher held the Bible over the pulpit like Rafiki holding Simba over the cliff in *The Lion King*, we knew that he was saying that the Bible was the authority.

The Bible was central to our faith. And though we might not have felt comfortable putting it this way, the Bible wasn't just central to our faith, it was the center of it. We spoke a lot of God, Jesus, and the Holy Spirit, but we all instinctively knew what everything in our faith rotated around: the Bible.

Our pastors, preachers, and teachers would never miss an opportunity to remind us that the Bible was perfect and without error, contradiction, or fault on any topic on which it chose to speak. And that "any topic on which it chose to speak" clause ended up being any and every topic: Science. Sexuality. Psychology. Social issues. Nothing ever seemed exempt from the Bible's perfect purview.

The Bible Is Fallible

I eventually learned that this doctrine had a name: *Inerrancy*. And while inerrancy-adherents quibble over the extent of inerrancy—for instance, is inerrancy limited only to the original manuscripts (which we don't have) or does it extend to the ones that we do have—the outcome is almost always the same: The Bible is the final authority and arbiter on literally everything, and it is never wrong.

The problem with this view, of course, is Jesus himself. I hate to be Debbie Downer here, but Jesus did not say, "All authority on heaven and on earth are given to the books that you are about to write." Jesus said, **"I HAVE BEEN GIVEN ALL AUTHORITY in heaven and on earth."**[3]

Jesus didn't have a Bible.

No one on the hillside listening to Jesus would ever see anything remotely resembling a Bible in their lifetime; the Bible wouldn't be compiled for a few more centuries. Nothing in the New Testament was written yet, and it wouldn't be written for decades, if not longer. It is unlikely any biblical author conceived that anything remotely resembling the Bible would ever come into existence. The earliest Christians didn't think that they would live long enough to need it.

It is clear from the biblical texts that the Apostles and authors of the New Testament expected Jesus to return in their lifetimes. They were not preparing for a day when the Apostles' voices would be silenced by death, so there was no grand plan to create or compile an authoritative document of doctrine, let alone an inerrant one.

While some have said that the Early Church passed around the earliest segments of the Bible like it was of equal weight and authority as we hold it today, the historical record doesn't seem to support the point. While the Early Church did increasingly view certain writings as more important than others, it did not hold them to be inerrant or authoritative, at least, not in the ways that we think of those words.

---

[3] Matthew 28:18.

For example, The Apostles' Creed—one of the earliest distillations of the core tenets of the Christian faith—doesn't hint at the presence or authority of any writings, biblical or otherwise, even though all of the Hebrew Scriptures existed and many or all of the writings that would eventually become the New Testament were in existence.

The later, and arguably even more significant, Nicene Creed is also absolutely silent on mentioning any writings as authoritative. The Creed of Chalcedon doesn't mention any writings either.

All of the early creeds are strangely silent, which makes no sense if the Early Church considered any of the 27 books of the New Testament to be as holy, important, sacred, authoritative, or necessary as we do today. And if the earliest Christians considered these texts to be the inerrant voice of God—a perfect word-for-word transcript from the Spirit of God—then their absolute silence makes no sense.

It is almost as if they intentionally ignore the authority of the writings that would become the Bible. Or, perhaps, it is that they understood that the Gospels, Epistles, and writings attest to *the thing*, but they aren't *the thing* itself. We know this because many of the Church Fathers within the Early Church did, indeed, write about, speak about, and hold dear these texts. But they did so without crossing a line that pushed these texts toward idolatry.

Inerrancy is idolatry, not orthodoxy.

The Early Church seemed to understand that the writings that would become the Bible were not the verbatim "Word of God"—that was Jesus—but that they were invaluable tools to help us navigate our way to Jesus and the God of the Hebrew Scriptures. The Early Church understood that these writings were amazing, beautiful, holy, and yes, even incredibly transformative, but God did not write them. Men wrote a book about God, and it somehow, wonderfully, mysteriously, breathes life into dead and dying things.

The thought of the Bible as mystery didn't scare me or threaten to destroy my faith. I had spent years in the Church studying the concept of faith, and isn't mystery an essential ingredient of faith? The thought of the Bible as a magnificent mystery was interesting to me. It was attractive in a way that ignited a longing deep within me to explore the texts more, and that was a long-dormant feeling that took me by surprise. The false idol of inerrancy had all but completely marred the beauty that I had once seen in the texts. Inerrancy had taken the mystery of the divine and straitjacketed it to human interpretation.

By making inerrancy my idol and elevating the biblical texts above their proper place, I realized that I had made the Bible the fourth member of the Trinity. At times, I had gone so far as to replace the Holy Spirit with the Bible. I had allowed the texts to be the voice of God in my life rather than the one whom God had sent to be an indwelling witness and confirmation of his will, the Spirit. I desired the texts of the Bible rather than the literal Spirit of God because I wanted to set into concrete what God had preferred to be complex and mysterious.

I swallowed deeply, the next thought stuck in my throat.

As hard as it was for me to admit, I think that somewhere along my journey I had become servant to the wrong master.

I lifted my head up to look at the cross again.

The concrete upon which I'd been kneeling had left its impression on my knees. I could *feel* the immovability of the cement against my skin.

And there it was, right in front of me, staring me in the face.

Christ is concrete; Christianity and the Bible are not.

Jesus Is Infallible

Jesus was inerrant, perfect, and without error.

The texts written about him were not inerrant, perfect, and without error … and that was okay.

That was okay, right?

I didn't need a perfect text about Jesus; I just needed Jesus.

If that be true, then I realized that having a complex, complicated, and nuanced relationship with the Bible was okay because the texts themselves were complex, complicated, and nuanced. If the point isn't perfection, then the power is in their purpose.

The purpose of scripture was to be the lighthouse in the harbor, pointing the way toward the cross that would lead me back to the Christ whom I had lost sight of during the storm that threatened to deconstruct my faith to the point of deconversion.

I instinctively knew that without something concrete—an anchor—I would likely not weather the spiritual storm. I needed to be tethered to something. For me, it couldn't be the Bible. I had too many questions; my trust issues were too great. I know many people tether themselves to the texts of scripture in these moments, but I wondered if those who remained concreted to the Bible instead of Christ truly weathered the storm of deconstruction.

I was convinced that this was the only path forward for my faith. I had to realign my life with the thinking of the Early Church. I knew that my anchor had to be Jesus.

Simply. Jesus.

And as foreign as it felt, there was a sense of calm in my spirit at the thought. There was hope in the idea that Christ was sufficient.

From a young age, I had been told that the Bible was sufficient. But I wasn't so sure anymore. Maybe I had been taught incorrectly.

A slight smile crept across my face as my mind wandered to the back row of my childhood church where we always sat. There I was, seven years old, my dad to my left and my grandfather's unmistakable white hair glowing five rows in front of me. The four rows between my Grandpa and me were filled with aunts, uncles, cousins, and extended family. For as long as I could remember, we had occupied these five rows. As a child, these people were my anchors. But love me as they do, they could no longer be my anchor.

My eyes welled with tears as I took another look at my grandfather; I miss him, a lot. He had been my anchor for so long. I willed my eyes out of focus to look beyond him. There, just beyond, was the pulpit that had oft been pounded with a Bible. By seven, I had heard many a hellfire-and-brimstone sermon from behind it. I would hear many more in the years to come, sitting center aisle, back row, left side. But as I stared at the pulpit that had been the central fixture of my childhood church experience, I noticed the wooden cross affixed to its front.

Had that always been there?!

The cross, right there, in front of the pulpit … in front of the pastor … in front of the Bible.

The cross.

Alone.

Not standing in the way of them, but standing in front of them.

The cross, which was now the center of my hope, the eye of my storm.

I stared at it for an eternity, considering the implications for my unrest. The sounds around me slowly silenced, and a hymn softly began to play in the theater of my mind, the song that we always sang as we waited for the Lord to move:

All to Jesus, I surrender,
Lord, I give myself to Thee,
Fill me with Thy love and power,
Let Thy blessings fall on me.

I stood up, absolutely dwarfed by the cross at the Abbey, but my feet firmly planted on the same concrete within which it grandly stood.

The cross and I, concreted together.

Looking up at the cross again, the sight took my breath away. For the first time, I noticed a dazzling curtain of sparkling lights surrounding it on all sides, behind it, to its left and right, and wrapping beyond the limits of my peripheral vision. Thousands of lights, perhaps millions, as brilliant or better than the stars in the sky.

Allowing my eyes to refocus, I realized that these thousands of points of light were not stars, but the light from countless homes stretching for miles up the York Valley and into the Allegheny Plateau beyond. Each home worked together to create a magnificent and impossibly magical curtain of lights that connected at the horizon to a billion more. All of this working together to make a spectacular display of grandeur. It was impossible to tell where the lights ended and the stars began.

Heaven and earth connected, behind the cross.

I realized that, though my time of prayer had ended for now, somewhere beyond the cross there were others, that very hour, who were continuing to pray … for me, for my church, for my wife and family, and for all of creation to have the same encounter with Jesus that I had just had at this cross.

Jesus had endured tremendous pain during the moments he hung on the cross, and perhaps, I could endure my own just a bit longer as well.

"... Let Thy blessings fall on me."

Reflect

1. If you grew up in a faith or church context, is there any tradition, song, or other piece of it that you still hold tightly to today?
2. What is one thing in life that you have elevated to a high position but that ended up letting you down?
3. Is there a person who has been an anchor for your spiritual journey over the years?
4. If the Bible isn't perfect but Jesus is, how does that affect you?
5. Do words like "All to Jesus, I surrender. All to him, I freely give" bring you comfort or peace? If they bring pain, can you explain why?

5 Deconstruct-Reconstruct Cycle

> If I ever become a Saint, I will surely be one of "darkness." I will continually be absent from Heaven—to light the light of those in darkness on Earth.
>
> —Mother Teresa

The Abbey of the Genesee is set on 2,400 picturesque acres in western New York that feature towering deciduous trees and forests criss-crossed by streams that empty in the nearby Genesee River, and eventually, Lake Erie; gently rolling hills; and endless fields of grain.

Everything has a purpose in the enclosure, which is the area of the monastery set aside only for the monks. The recently harvested grain from the fields, for instance, will soon be baked into bread at the Abbey and sold on-site, online, and across the Northeast as "Monk's Bread." This is how the Trappist Monks support themselves and the Abbey, by bread-making.

There is something poetic about leaving the cross and finding myself in the middle of fields that are a nursery for bread, a symbol so tied to the heart of Jesus.

This do in remembrance of me.

It is across these fields that I must make my way in order to arrive at my lodging for the week. The path is a haphazardly mown walkway of grass that meanders its way along the countryside, across two creeks and several aging wooden bridges, before eventually arriving at Bethlehem Retreat House. “Bethlehem”—the monks shorten the name of the Retreat House to one word—is the Abbey’s primary lodging for the multitude of pilgrims who come from around the world each year seeking hope, healing, or spiritual health at the Abbey.

For me, it was all three.

It was dark, and I had yet to unpack my flashlight, so the half-mile journey from the cross to Bethlehem was going to have to be made by moonlight. I wondered if I had made a serious mistake by parking my car for the week, locking my cell phone inside, and eschewing transportation and digital connection in an attempt to live as the monks and avoid distractions.

Like the monks who lived in silent contemplation, I was determined to spend a week listening rather than talking. I hoped that quieting my surroundings would quiet my soul enough to hear the voice of God loud enough to figure out how to follow it again.

Like the old "Marco Polo" game children sometimes play in swimming pools, I believed that hearing God's voice again, just once, even faintly, would give me enough strength to find him, even in the dark.

I just needed to avoid drowning.

As a pastor who spends almost all of their waking hours in a church, it was an odd thing to admit that I had stopped hearing the voice of God. The feeling of disconnection was not just disconcerting, it was soul-crushing. It isn't a problem that a lot of people are willing to openly admit, but I knew that I was not alone. After her death, Mother Teresa's writings revealed that she had endured five decades without feeling the presence of God.[1]

I didn't want to go that long disconnected.

I knew that I *couldn't* go that long disconnected.

Mother Teresa may be able to endure 50 years in a dark night of the soul, but I am no Mother Teresa.

My runway was running out.

As I traversed the well-worn path between the cross and Bethlehem, I wondered where I might find help for my newfound flicker of hope. If the Bible was not it, then where?

The church?

I am a pastor, and yet that thought of trying to find hope in the walls of the church still sent a shudder down my spine. Four decades of involvement in multiple churches and denominations—two decades of which were spent in staff and pastoral roles—had convinced me that the church was probably the last place I would find a path forward for my faith.

And I am not alone in my concern that the American church has largely failed in its efforts to draw people to God and be the hands and feet of Jesus in this generation.

---

[1] Mother Teresa, *Come Be My Light: The Private Writings of the Saint of Calcutta* (Doubleday, 2007).

The Origins of the Failure

The church has a problem, and it isn't the culture, the world, or Christians who want to sin rather than follow God. Approximately 70% of teenagers drop out of church and stop practicing their faith during the transition from adolescence to adulthood.[2] Unlike previous generations, these individuals are not returning to the church in their late twenties to forties as they start families. The effect is a radical reduction in church participation and an age-imbalance in the pews. Author and evangelical researcher David Kinnaman has given years to researching the problem, and he blames the church itself, boldly and bluntly stating, "the institutionalized church has failed."[3]

Those who leave and don't return are simply referred to as "Dones." And data indicates that their children tend to become "Nones," people who have never had any religious affiliation and are unlikely to ever become a part of a religious faith.

But this doesn't mean that the Dones and Nones have no spiritual faith. It simply means that they are unwilling to practice their faith as part of a traditional local church congregation or organized denominational structure.

This is an understandable problem for the church. A generation, or more, of people who practice their faith apart from the church could be catastrophic to the current institutional church,

[2] For a broader treatment, see Thomas E. Bergler, *The Juvenilization of American Christianity* (Grand Rapids, MI: Eerdmans, 2012); Christian Stephen Smith and Melinda Lundquist Denton, *Soul Searching: The Religious and Spiritual Lives of American Teenagers* (New York: Oxford University Press, 2009); and David Kinnaman and Aly Hawkins, *You Lost Me: Why Young Christians Are Leaving Church … and Rethinking Faith* (Grand Rapids, MI: Baker, 2011).
[3] David Kinnaman and Gabe Lyons, *Unchristian: What a New Generation Really Thinks about Christianity—And Why It Matters* (Grand Rapids, MI: Baker, 2007), 11.

whose buildings, programs, and staff salaries rely on strong attendance and giving. Further, many Evangelical churches and leaders exert an inordinate amount of power in politics and the public square.

But to think about the health of the church above—and often at the expense of—the individual has proven disastrous.

The problem for local church congregations, though, is that they have invested so much into the institutional church, it seems nearly impossible to pivot and center the individual over the system. Today, when people hear the word *church*, they don't imagine a person as much as buildings, infrastructures, denominations, and religious organizations. And we have been investing in that institution-over-individual mindset for a long time in the United States.

Many look to the post–World War II era for insight into the American church and how it lost its way. After the war, the church experienced explosive and ongoing growth in power, prominence, and number of converts, building increasingly larger church buildings and more powerful religious institutions, but the momentum could not be maintained. The Silent generation leveraged this growth, building increasingly larger church buildings and powerful religious institutions. But the momentum was short-lived.

The religious headwinds began to shift in the 1960s and 1970s, and then accelerated into the 1980s and 1990s as scandals rocked the church and political influence became a goal within Evangelicalism. As attendance began to wane, the church had difficulty adjusting to the new normal and has never quite recovered. The trends continue unabated.

The Building versus the People

Perhaps most problematic to its recovery, the modern church tends to see itself as more of a *building* than a *people*. This encourages the elevation of the institution over the individual, which creates enormous issues in return. When in conflict, this mindset makes it easy for pastors and boards to protect the institution rather than the individual.

For instance, many of the mishandled cases of sexual abuse in the church were directly attributable to religious leaders choosing to protect the interests of the institution, even if it meant coverups, no admission of guilt, lack of cooperation with authorities, and even victim blaming. These were seen as acceptable solutions to protect the institution because of all the supposed good that it had otherwise accomplished. But these kinds of situational ethics aren't limited to sexual abuse allegations. Situational ethics play themselves out every day in church financial decisions, hiring/firing of staff, church discipline, and a plethora of other decisions at all levels.

Protecting the institution, at any cost, can easily become the sole focus of pastors and church leaders whenever a church is in crisis, as though the institution *is* the church. But we must admit that it is not, if we are being honest with the biblical texts.

The institution *is not* the church, neither is the building.

The English word *church* is translated from the New Testament Greek word *ekklesia*. Because of the context in which it is used in multiple New Testament books—not to mention its standard usage in everyday Greek—we can confidently say that the *ekklesia* ("church") is a people, not a place.

Ekklesia is a compound of two words: *ek* ("out") and *kaleo* ("to call"), a group of people who are called out from a larger group. An *ekklesia* is a group of "called out ones" or "a gathering of those called."

When we see the word *church* in our English Bibles, we should insert the word *ekklesia* instead, imagining a group of all the people who are followers of The Way of Jesus.

People, not a building.

So, for instance, whenever Jesus says in the Gospel of Matthew, "I will build my church, and all the powers of hell will not conquer it,"[4] he is saying that the realm of the dead (i.e., Hades) will never overtake those who are his called out ones (i.e., "my church/*ekklesia*"). This verse is making a statement about the people, not an institution.

This works similarly for another biblical text from the Book of Hebrews that has often been abused to imply that the church is an institution or a place, not just a people.

> *Let us think of ways to motivate one another to acts of love and good works. And let us not neglect our meeting together, as some people do, but encourage one another. . . .*[5]

Many pastors—including myself during the early years of ministry—have bent this biblical text to mean that a Christ-follower must attend a Sunday worship gathering, in a building, as part of a sanctioned church or be in violation of God's command to not forsake gathering with the official assembly. But the Greek text and broader context of the chapter indicates that the point of this text isn't a command to attend church. The author's intent here is to discourage new followers of Christ from avoiding spending time with other followers of Jesus because everyone needed to be encouraged so no one drifted away from their new faith.

The point was: "Be in conversation and community with other followers of The Way" and not so much "Be in church every Sunday."

---

[4] Matthew 16:18.

[5] Hebrews 10:24–25a.

So, yes, an institutional church *can* fulfill the purpose of Hebrews 10, but it doesn't *have* to. It's not the only way. Any gathering of Christ-followers for encouragement toward greater love and action will do. If a church building's gathering does not promote encouragement and greater love of Christ, other believers, and the broader community, then the author of Hebrews would likely encourage us to find a group of Christians somewhere that *do* accomplish those things.

As difficult as that reality is for pastors and leaders of institutional churches to admit, we must be honest with what the texts say … and especially what the texts *don't* say. And to be blunt, many institutional church gatherings have done more to push people away from the faith than draw them more deeply into it.

When we force the *ekklesia* to be a place rather than a people, we do immeasurable harm to the people of God.

And that is a problem we must face head-on.

Pastors, like me, have long blamed cultural trends and the influence of "the world" on the downturn in Sunday morning attendance numbers, and the rise of the Dones and Nones, but the data seems to indicate that the real problem isn't outside of the walls of our church buildings but inside them.

In short, the reality of flagging attendance, and perhaps, even flagging faith, is caused by the church itself.

It is understandable that pastors and church leaders would rather avoid owning the issue. No one likes admitting a problem when you have no clue what caused it or how to solve it.

I stopped dead in my tracks, somewhere on the walking path between the Abbey and the Retreat House. I was overwhelmed by the darkness.

Yes, I was overwhelmed by the expansive darkness of the night as it enveloped me in the middle of the field, but I was also overwhelmed by the inner darkness that I felt in having played a role in religious systems that had brought pain to others. As a pastor, I had spent years representing and serving the church, an institution that had perpetrated harm on others.

I contributed to the current predicament.

I need to admit that.

There, in the middle of a random grass path, in the middle of an open Abbey field, in the middle of Nowhere, New York, I realized that it would be impossible for me to move forward in my journey unless I could admit my failures and own the problems of the greater church.

So, I acknowledged my failures and problems with the following:

I CONFESS that I

- Often lost my way as a pastor of God's people.
- Regularly cared more for the people inside than out.
- Long misunderstood the mission of the people of God.
- Often held the place as more important than the people.
- Espoused and taught harmful doctrines about the church.
- Often protected the interests of the institution at the expense of the people.

I looked up into the stars above me, tears streaming down my face, to God, to all whom I had brought any harm or pain:

I am sorry.
Forgive me, if you can.

The question in my mind was: Could I forgive *myself*?

Cycles of Deconstruction and Reconstruction Are Healthy

Once I saw the problem and admitted the reality of the decline, I couldn't unsee it … or forget it. You don't lose 70% of your youth year over year, and not see it reflected in the pews and general momentum of the broader church. I knew that if we didn't figure out the problem and face it, there would be no end to the rise of the Dones and Nones.

Transparently, I had no issue with people choosing a life without faith. I was only called to share the good news of Jesus. Faith cannot be forced. But I had a very real problem with people choosing to walk away from Jesus because they felt like they were left no choice. How could the church live with itself if people rejected Jesus and his way of life because the church turned them off to it?

As a father, it was even more personal. If the church continued its current decline, then three of my four children would walk away from the faith themselves.

We should have seen this coming, though. Five decades ago when the church still seemed to be growing in numbers and power, sociologist Robert Bellah warned of treacherous headwinds: "The cultural vitality in America of several religious traditions has been waning for a long time."[6]

At the time, few wanted to believe that the church was in crisis, so Bellah and other wise voices were mostly ignored. It is easy to understand why the church has had such difficulty coming to terms with the reality of its situation. Things had been so good for so long that it seemed the institutional church could not be stopped.

---

[6]Robert Bellah, *The Broken Covenant: American Civil Religion in a Time of Trial* (New York: Seabury Press, 1975), 109.

But before we count out the people of God, the church has been at this crossroads before … a lot. The entirety of the church's 2,000-year history has been one long series of advancements and setbacks. Ups and downs. One step forward; two steps back, or twenty.

To only see the church through the lens of the last few decades is to miss the greater story of God at work, a story of beauty (and peril) that doesn't perfectly arc across its 20th-century trajectory, but, instead, acts like a roller coaster along 2,000 years of wild ups and downs of progress and regress.

Yes, the church is in a period of difficulty that should not be ignored, but if we look closely to the past, we see that the church seems to have a pattern of (re)formation after extended periods of difficulty. That is hope! The most recent reformation was a relatively recent 500 years ago during (I love that we call it this) the Great Reformation.

By the late 1400s, the church looked rather deformed in comparison to how it had once looked during the days of the Early Church. While many problems plagued the church, it is safe to say that it had become over-institutionalized and had drifted far in both faith and practice. Men like Martin Luther, John Calvin, and Ulrich Zwingli sought to reconstruct something different than the church of the previous generation. What emerged was a reformation of the church.

While some might quibble as to whether the results of the Great Reformation were better or worse than the version of the church that led to it, we must admit that both sides benefitted from the reformation, not just the newly created Protestant movement. The process of reformation from the deformation in the Catholic Church led to its own reformation within Roman Catholicism as well.

Sometimes, something needs to be broken apart in order to be made new.

This isn't the only time this has happened, though. Roughly 500 years before the Great Reformation, the church was locked in another similar conflict after a period of struggle between the Patriarch of Constantinople and the Pope of Rome. A thousand years later, it is difficult to understand how fierce the conflict was! While there were several issues that caused the furor, one of the foremost concerns was whether the communion bread should be leavened (with yeast) or unleavened (without). The Pope said unleavened; the Patriarch said leavened. Thus, the Great Schism between the Western (Catholic) and Eastern (Orthodox) Churches in the 11th century led to a split and subsequent reconstruction of two different religious institutions that went their separate ways … over bread.

Never let it be said that the meal doesn't matter.

If you are expecting another great difficulty in the church, you would be correct. Almost as if on time, 500 years before the Great Schism of the 11th century (which was 500 years before the previous one), the church endured another deconstruction and reconstruction over the nature of Christ and his mother Mary. The flashpoint happened at the Council of Chalcedon in the 6th century, and it led to the Oriental Orthodox churches splitting from the Eastern and Western Churches, which, of course, were united at the time. These Oriental Orthodox congregations—better known today as the Coptic Orthodox, Syriac Orthodox, Armenian Apostolic, Indian Syrian Orthodox, and Ethiopian Orthodox Churches—disconnected themselves over doctrine and reconstructed in order to follow the path upon which they felt the Spirit was leading them.

Writer and poet Phyllis Tickle first pointed out these periods of deformation and (re)formation in her book *The Great*

Emergence.[7] In it, she reminds the reader that, while it may be impossible to fully feel the emotions that went into each upheaval, each difficulty may be helpful as we think of our modern-day issues in the church.

It doesn't take a math major or history PhD to see that these breakdowns and (re)formings in the church have come, almost like clockwork, every 500 years—451 CE, 1054 CE, and 1517 CE. If history truly does repeat itself, the church is on schedule to experience its fourth reformation, having just celebrated the 500th anniversary of the last Great Reformation several years ago.

Depending on what one has to gain or lose, a deconstruction of the church and subsequent reconstruction into something new could be the worst or best news ever.

Tickle points out that, while the upheaval of deconstruction can feel like the death of something critical to the faith, history has shown us that each of these reconstructions didn't destroy the church. Far from it, each Deconstruction-Reconstruction Cycle led to a renewed stability in the church, each lasting for five centuries.

It might even be said that without a deep and total deconstruction, the church would have ceased to exist. Or, at least, it would have ceased to have been as effective. Each cycle breathed new life into the church.

The Deconstruction-Reconstruction Cycle was necessary to the church's health and mission. Tickle reminds us that the very history of our faith proves that when an overly institutionalized version of Christianity is battered into pieces and opened to the world around it, whatever is left in the end has spread and changed the world for the better.

---

[7] Phyllis Tickle, *The Great Emergence: How Christianity Is Changing and Why* (Grand Rapids, MI: Baker Books, 2012).

If the church can, and has, deconstructed and reconstructed in order to form a lasting faith, it made sense to me that a follower of Christ could also benefit from dismantling the parts of their faith that were counterproductive in order to (re)construct a faith capable of facing whatever was next on the journey.

Whatever was *next on the journey*?

I looked up just in time to see the lights of the Bethlehem Retreat House in front of me. I had made it through the dark journey, and the thought of a church changed for the better excited me. The idea that it could be rebuilt from the rubble of broken pieces gave me hope.

If the church had risen time and again from difficulty, perhaps I could as well.

The thought of a world changed for the better hung in my head as the lights of Bethlehem loomed closer and closer.

The half-hour walk from the foot of the cross, and then across the fields to Bethlehem, had me laughing. It felt backward, like traveling in reverse. The order was all wrong; I chuckled to myself. Bethlehem to the cross, not the cross to Bethlehem!

And yet here I was, moving forward by going into the past.

That thought sat with me.

I was beginning to sense that, were I to ever find a path forward, it would only be found by stepping into the past.

Perhaps, rather than trying to reconstruct something new out of the broken pieces of my faith, I needed to reconstruct something old.

Reflect

1. What parts of the current church need to be deconstructed?
2. Are there things in life, or the church, that should never be taken apart and rebuilt?
3. If you had to list the top three things the church does currently, what would they be?
4. Can you think of another business or program that had to deconstruct and reconstruct to stay alive?
5. What is the main difference, in your mind, between the church in the Bible and the church in reality?

PART II

Reconstructing Faith

6 Ancient Paths

> Marty, the future isn't written. It can be changed. You know that. Anyone can make their future whatever they want it to be.
>
> —Doc Brown, *Back to the Future III*

When I arrived at the Abbey, the half-mile footpath between the cross and Bethlehem was mown but mostly unused. It seemed to be more of a suggestion than a serious alternative to the road nearby. But having set aside all of my mobile technology—including my car—for the week, I had firmly committed myself to the footpath.

Was I stubborn? Yes.

Was I going to pretend that I enjoyed walking even when it was miserably cold, raining, seemingly endless, and completely unnecessary? Also, yes.

I was the only person who took the walking path that week. I never passed anyone on the foot journey to or from the Abbey.

I must have seemed like the oddest pilgrim to the other retreat guests who drove back and forth, accomplishing in three minutes what took me thirty, at best.

I would occasionally catch a glimpse of them driving by as their road criss-crossed my path. They never seemed very happy to me … or free.

The Abbey's seven daily services—yes, *seven* daily services—were spread throughout the day, and night, which meant that I spent as much time on the journey to worship as I did in worship. Over time, an odd thing began to occur. I was worshipping as much on the footpath as I was in the pew. I began to look forward to the services being over so that the worship could begin, in God's great cathedral of creation itself.

I spent so much time treading the path between Bethlehem and the Abbey, that the footpath began to carry visible scars from my journey as it wore down to dirt from my repeated footfalls, the once beautiful grass giving way to the mud and muck beneath.

It was dirt to one person's eyes, but to another, rich farming soil made perfect for bread-grain. Dirt that I now carried on my shoes and body as a visible reminder to having taken the road less traveled each day on my way to the cross.

Had I not taken the more difficult path, though, I am uncertain as to whether I would have found my way back to faith.

With each advancing hour spent alone on the path, my soul began to unwind and disconnect from the anxiety of the storm in my soul and still-stalled spiritual life. Each step forward in the dirt began to feel less and less like I was walking away from something, and more and more as though I was walking toward something.

Something important.

Something rooted.

Something sacred.

In the Hebrew Scriptures, there is an ancient prophet by the name of Jeremiah who had the very unenviable job of being the voice of God among a group of people who didn't seem to want to listen. Jeremiah pleads with the people, but their ears were closed. The text, sadly and somewhat humorously, remarks that not only are the people unashamed, but *"they don't even know how to blush"* about it.[1]

And yet, despite the tragic past through which they had come because of their own broken ways, God still offered a way forward. This is what Jeremiah said to the people on behalf of God:

Stand at the crossroads and look;
ask for the ancient paths,
ask where the good way is, and walk in it,
and you will find rest for your souls.[2]

As a longtime Protestant who somehow found himself on a "Hail Mary" of a spiritual retreat in a Catholic monastery, the word *ancient* struck a nerve with me.

I just couldn't get past it.

[1]Jeremiah 6:15.

[2]Jeremiah 6:16b, NIV.

Rediscovering the Roots

All of the spiritually formative contexts in which I had been raised and trained took a rather dim view of anything ancient. Growing up, *ancient* was an organ, a hymnal, and a 1611 KJV Bible.

Our idea of ancient clearly had its limits. To us, the true church began in the New Testament, then skipped forward to sometime around the Great Reformation in the early 1500s. What happened in between was viewed as somewhere on a continuum between unimportant and ungodly.

I had been taught to distrust Catholicism—or any tradition, for that matter—that extended more than 500 years into the past. That meant that saints were unhelpful (and a sin to celebrate), praying written prayers didn't count (and angered God), and things like Confirmation were the devil's tool to trick people into believing they weren't headed for hell (which they were, to us, of course, as were most Protestants other than us).

I was raised firmly Fundamentalist, if you had not already noticed.

As I grew up, I began to question the validity of many things that I had been taught as a child about other Christians and their spiritual practices. I quickly realized that my Fundamentalism was fraught with inconsistencies. But it wasn't until my time immersed at the Abbey that I realized the true extent of this error.

We never noticed our own blind spots and contradictions. We insisted that our doctrines and practices—unlike the Catholic Church—perfectly matched the doctrines and practices of the Early Church, but this couldn't have been further from the truth. We were blissfully ignorant of church history, deceiving ourselves into believing that other, more ancient forms of formation could never have the power to transform?

We would have never been able to admit the possibility that other, older ways of faith formation may have been even better at transformation than our own. Perhaps if we could have recognized that our forms of faith formation had directly come from these ancient ways—still largely practiced by Catholic, Orthodox, and other adherents around the world—then we might have been able to consider their value.

We had become disconnected from our roots. And like the people to whom Jeremiah ministered, we needed to consider ancient paths, long forgotten, in order to move forward.

I began to desperately desire pastors and leaders who would, like Jeremiah, stand up and shout:

> … *ask for the ancient paths, ask where the good way is, and walk in it, and you will find rest for your souls. …*

But I must admit, even if a leader in my Evangelical stream had done such a thing, I fear that most of the Christians around me would have replied:

> … *We will not walk in it!*[3]

This matters.

And, it mattered to me … spiritually.

My heart was torn. I was finding peace for my soul in ancient rhythms that I knew would not be acceptable by those around me. I instinctively knew that were I to walk an ancient path in order to find my faith, I would walk it alone.

I wondered if this was what happened to Jeremiah. Was there no one walking the ancient paths because no one was willing to walk them alone?

As my time at the Abbey progressed through the warp and woof of ancient worship and uncomfortable immersion in

---

[3] Jeremiah 6:16, NIV.

Early Church tools of spiritual formation, my soul began to find rest.

Jeremiah was right, at least, for me.

Ancient paths brought rest for my soul; I found it to be a "good way," so I walked in it.

There, in the Abbey, for the first time, I was confronted with the power of a practice-based faith. The religious contexts of my past had always relied on logic, ration, and apologetics to convince the mind, which would hopefully form faith. The "transformation of the mind"[4] was taken literally in that once a heart-decision had occurred, the rest of a Christian's journey should be focused on right belief rather than right practice … or much of any practice at all. The thought was that "right belief" would lead to "right practice."

But there we were, thinking again.

The Abbey opened my eyes to the opposite side of the coin, a world where "practice" led to "belief," rather than the other way around. I was introduced to a world where immersing oneself in ancient spiritual practices might better form one into a follower of The Way than the latest, greatest discipleship fad imported from the megachurch down the road.

It shouldn't be shocking to assume that practices proven effective for centuries, even millennia, might work, but it *was* shocking.

Theologian and author Leonard Sweet has long advocated for this kind of thinking in faith formation. Sweet calls for a faith formation model that is more E.P.I.C. in nature, seeing it as far more biblically—and scientifically—defensible:[5]

---

[4] Romans 12:2.

[5] For more on the E.P.I.C. framework, see Leonard Sweet, *Post-Modern Pilgrims: First-Century Passion for the 21st-Century Church* (Nashville, TN: B&H Academic, 2000); and Leonard Sweet, *The Gospel According to Starbucks: Living with a Grande Passion* (Colorado Springs, CO: Waterbrook, 2007).

- **Experiential:** Moving beyond rational belief and propositional statements of belief and doctrine to helping others *experience* the truth of a living Jesus in their everyday lives, in a way, drives right living over perfect belief.
- **Participatory:** Moving from *taking apart* to instead *taking part in* a journey, turning the person into an active author who initiates and participates in their journey of formation, rather than passively listening and observing.
- **Image-rich:** Moving beyond words on a page (or dare I say, Bible) to imagery. Moving from mere words to bringing thoughts to life using metaphors, the five senses, and emotions to see and experience the *living* presence of Christ.
- **Connective:** Humans are relational beings and are desperate for connection with creation, others, culture, their community, and the Divine. When people are invited to connect with others, they are also being invited to connect with the transcendent.[6]

At the Abbey, I rediscovered a plethora of powerful ancient tools that began to breathe back life into my faith like bellows do warm embers, fanning it into a raging wildfire that could barely be contained or controlled.

Of course, I say "rediscovered," but I admit that these E.P.I.C. ancient practices are not new and have been practiced by millions, uninterrupted, since the Early Church began using them to form faith nearly 2,000 years ago.

Though the Evangelical churches of my childhood, college, seminary, and pastorates had mostly shunned all of these ancient practices that I was now immersing myself into, they had withstood the test of time, proving themselves to be effective tools of formation since the early days of Christianity.

---

[6]Adapted from: Leonard Sweet, *Giving Blood: A Fresh Paradigm for Preaching* (Grand Rapids, MI: Zondervan, 2014), 46–57.

And now they were forming me … in the span of days, not years or decades.

The History of the Church Can Teach Us Anew

As I came to learn, it made sense that these ancient practices would find so much effectiveness in this particular day and age. The difficult social and cultural situation in which the Early Church found itself was not unlike the situation in which the church finds itself today. If the cultures are similar, then it shouldn't surprise us that more ancient ways may once again be the best way to form faith.

At the dawn of the Early Church, few if any serious individuals would have bet the farm on Christianity lasting more than a few decades, let alone its eventual domination of the entire Roman Empire.

As the age of the New Testament passed with Peter, John, and the Apostles, the church entered adolescence facing serious questions. Who would lead, and how would this fledgling religious movement keep from being numbered among the multitude of religious cults that shriveled and died in the absence of their dynamic founders?

A close read of the New Testament writings reveal that the earliest Christians expected Jesus to return before the death of the Apostles. They expected his soon return … *very* soon. There was no long-term plan in place.

Adding to their concern was the very real and literal struggle for survival within a highly secularized society that was becoming increasingly hostile to followers of The Way of Jesus. As the second generation of Christ-followers took the handoff from the Apostles, the church found itself with little power, political or otherwise, limited resources, and a notable lack of leadership.

The great Apostles had passed, and with them, the hope of a soon return.

If Christianity were to survive, it would have to invest heavily in the formation of deep faith within the next generation of Christians. Until now, followers had been directly formed by Jesus or an Apostle (or under an Apostle's authority and oversight).

Fearing the effects of a generation of followers with unformed or malformed faith, the church believed that its best hope for survival was the formation of the mind and heart of Christ in each and every follower of The Way. The church hoped that these well-formed followers would, in turn, be able to adequately pass along the faith of The Fathers to another generation that would, again, continue the cycle generation after generation.

Why so much intensity and intentionality?

Adequate faith formation was an absolute necessity, in large part, due to the often messy backgrounds of the earliest converts to Christianity. In the past—during the New Testament era—converts to The Way had primarily come from Jewish and God-fearing Gentile backgrounds. This meant that the Apostles and Bishops of the New Testament era could build upon the religious foundations that were already in place. Early adopters of The Way found Christianity to be a mostly logical extension of their Jewish rituals, routines, and beliefs. Much of early Christianity reflected familiar parts of Judaism, with the addition of Jesus' teachings.

But by the mid-2nd century—a mere century or so after Christ—the makeup of those being drawn to the Christian faith had greatly changed. Most converts to Christianity now came from places completely outside the reach of Judaism. New converts arrived in early Christian gatherings with allegiances to multiple gods, morally indifferent, and with little or no background knowledge of Jesus or the Judaism from which he came.

If The Way of Jesus was to survive more than a generation or two, it had to find a way to deprogram highly pagan converts and then reform them into fully devoted followers of Jesus.

Deprogram → (Re)program

Deconstruct → (Re)construct

The intentional reconstruction of a new Christ-follower's mind and heart was crucial if there was to be any hope of the church functioning as a countercultural movement. Suffice it to say, their efforts were dramatically successful.

Not only did the Christian faith survive this tumultuous era, it also thrived in a way that might be called miraculous. The rise of Christianity dealt an enormous blow to the secular institutions and belief systems of Late Antiquity, and Christianity's turnaround from a people oppressed by the Roman Empire to fully sanctioned as the faith of the Empire in less than four centuries was due, almost single-handedly, to the church's intentional training methods and immersion of its people into spiritual practices.

Follow Jesus' Lead

Using spiritual practices to form faith shouldn't really come as much of a surprise. Jesus himself participated in many various spiritual practices during his ministry, including solitude, prayer retreats, pilgrimage, fellowship, teaching, sacraments, worship, and many more.

Jesus' example should give us the courage to move beyond the false idea that rational deliberation on ideas and beliefs is the primary way that faith is formed, or even the best way. Jesus shows us that there are far better ways to form deep faith than to memorize and regurgitate doctrine.

For example, Jesus often used the journey from one place to another as an opportunity to teach. He immersed his followers in a practice-based faith that dismantled everything that they thought they knew about God and reconstructed it into something that transformed them from the inside out and overflowed into the communities around them.

Those closest to Jesus couldn't help but be impacted as much by his teaching as they were his life.

His earliest followers didn't just learn from him, they *experienced* him. They were often close enough to him to have been able to see the dust on his feet and dirty clothes from his travels.

Imagine being close enough to Jesus to see his dirty feet! I longed for that kind of immersion into The Way of Jesus and the Early Church.

There is a passage in the Jewish Mishnah—a collection of rabbinic writings from around and before the time of Jesus—that contains a line from Yose ben Yoezer:

> *Let thy house be a meeting-house for the wise;*
> *and powder thyself in the dust of their feet;*
> *and drink their words with thirstiness.*[7]

In the years that followed its writing, many rabbis and their disciples discussed the meaning of this passage. Some saw it as a statement intended to communicate the importance of sitting at the feet of a rabbi in order to learn, as many rabbis sat on dirt floors in order to teach. Others saw it as a statement on the need to follow a rabbi closely enough to be dusted by the dirt his feet kick up, or said differently, to be close enough to be influenced by your rabbi.

---

[7] *Pirkei Avot* 1:4 (Charles Taylor, trans.). https://sacred-texts.com/jud/sjf/sjf03.htm.

As I walked back and forth between Bethlehem and the cross, I longed to do more than just know Jesus. I wanted to truly experience him. I wanted to be close enough to him to be covered in his dust. Sitting at his feet was no longer enough for me.

With each footfall across the increasingly deconstructed dirt path of the Abbey grounds, I was becoming more and more covered in the dirt and mud as the result of my dedication to the path.

I was now certain that my feet were following Jesus' path. I was covered in the dust of Jesus' feet, close enough to be influenced by him again. Somehow, I had stumbled back onto The Way.

There, mid-hike between Bethlehem and the cross, I paused, the late autumn wind picked up around me, blowing leaves, remnants of the grain harvest, and dirt all around me.

Here, in the whirlwind, I knew that it was time.

All there was left to do was to allow him to reconstruct whatever he willed within me. I had given up control of what the future looked like. *What* was reconstructed was no longer as important to me as it was that *something* be reconstructed.

I wanted *something* instead of *nothing*.

There I stood, watching the wind blow the dirt and debris down the path behind me.

I turned to look ahead.

The cross before me, the dirt behind me.

No turning back.

I took my first step forward.

Reflect

1. Are there any spiritual practices that *have* brought you peace over the years?
2. In the E.P.I.C. framework (experiential, participatory, image-rich, connective), which of the four resonate most deeply with you?
3. How long do you predict that the church as we know it will exist? Why?
4. When you look at Jesus, what things do you see that are transferrable to your daily life?
5. Whose dust would you most like to be covered in, and why?

7 The Liturgy of the Hours

Pray without ceasing.

—Paul, the Apostle

I sat, silent, with my head in my hands. An expanse of pew extended to my left, and, to my right, empty save for me. The clock on my wrist said the hour was half-past 2:00 a.m. Not 30 minutes before, I had dragged my body from yet another night of restless slumber in order to, once again, make the half-mile walk from the Retreat House to the Abbey.

The Abbey holds seven services for worship and prayer each day, spread across the day and night, *every* day and night. When I had committed to immersing myself into the rhythms of the Abbey, I had not anticipated that the prayer rhythms of worship would wreck my sleep schedule. I had come to the Abbey to find rest for my soul, but the monks seemed intent on ensuring that I spent my time seated in a pew praying instead.

Looking around, it was impossible not to notice that all of the pews were empty, again, except the one that I was currently keeping warm. Out of the dozens of individuals on spiritual retreat at the Abbey, I was the only one who attended the 2:00 a.m. prayers, not just that night, but all week.

Admittedly, I was more than a little annoyed than I probably should have been that the only Protestant person in a Catholic Retreat House was the sole attendee at the daily 2:00 a.m. time of prayer, which they called *Vigils*.

Where was everyone?

Perhaps, as a Protestant, I had a lot of catching up to do.

So each evening, after only a couple of hours of sleep, I wrestled myself out of slumber into something resembling wakefulness in order to make my nightly vigil to the Abbey. Just me, the darkness, and the unsettling fear of what might be hiding in plain sight in the darkness.

As I trudged along the path, only half-awake, I pressed down these fears and kept my eyes upon the horizon, knowing that at some point along the way the lights of the Abbey would come into view.

The Devotion to Prayer

The Early Church knew a thing or two about darkness. Imagine the feeling of loneliness that must have settled into followers of The Way after their leader's surprise ascension and then the passing of the Apostles, one by one.

What now? they must have wondered.

As if all that weren't enough, competing religious movements and institutions were feeling threatened by this small but growing religious sect that was desperately seeking to follow Jesus' teachings. Even the secular ruling elite in Rome were joining the religious opposition in an attempt to fully eradicate followers of

The Way. Rumors of intensifying persecution and even imprisonments were beginning to become common table talk. Soon, Christians would be burned at the stake and fed to lions as sport. If the fledgling faith of Jesus, Peter, and Paul were to have any hope of survival, these early Christians needed a miracle.

Tough times call for intense prayer.

This is likely why the early Christians spent so much of their time focusing on the practice of prayer. When nothing else can be done, prayer often becomes the practice of last resort. But for them, prayer wasn't just a quick mealtime blessing or bedtime appetizer. Prayer was an important and necessary component of their daily rhythms, even before the difficulty of persecution arrived on their doorstep.

But let's not get too ahead of ourselves.

It should come as no surprise that the earliest followers of Jesus found prayer to be one of the most important and life-giving spiritual practices to which to devote themselves. Their founder, Jesus, famously spent a great deal of time and energy in prayer. And lest we lull ourselves into thinking that Jesus' prayers were always perfect pictures of hope and ease, they were not.

For example, pay close attention to Jesus' words in the Gospel of Matthew the night that he was facing betrayal and trial. In the passage, he openly admits that his "soul is very sorrowful, even to death." So what does he do? He asks a few of his closest friends, "Watch with me … and pray."[1]

In a crisis, Jesus prayed.

Of all the things that he could have possibly done, he prayed.

Even more remarkable, if we understand Jesus to be God, is that God prayed to himself.

---

[1] Matthew 26:38–41.

But I noticed something more in the words of his prayer, something that I had never noticed before: Jesus prayed pain-filled prayers! Sit with that for a moment. Let it sink in. Jesus prayed prayers that were just as tough and painful as mine … as yours.

There is so much more to find if we will only dig just a bit deeper. Times of turmoil were not the only times that Jesus prayed, far from it. If the biblical record is to be believed, then Jesus was almost always praying, in good times *and* in hard times … and all times in between.

When we start digging into Jesus' prayer routines, we find more than just a life committed to the power and practice prayer, we find a rhythm to his prayer.

Jesus didn't just pray a lot; Jesus prayed according to a schedule!

This matters.

For me, this discovery changed everything.

While the idea that Jesus had specific times during the day that he set aside in order to pray may seem revolutionary to us, it was normal for the time. So normal, in fact, that people around Jesus would not have thought much of it. Many Jews of Jesus' day—especially religious leaders, teachers, and rabbis—followed some pattern of regular prayer. It was such a common practice that the authors of scripture seemed to see little reason to point it out. It was assumed that readers of the Gospels and Letters would understand that every Jewish person prayed according to a prayer schedule, so there would have been no need to point it out or draw attention to it.

A prayer routine was an expectation of those most committed to God.

The practice was established well before Jesus. New Testament prayer practices found their inspiration in a number of excellent examples from the Hebrew Scriptures. One of the clearest was Daniel, the guy who got himself thrown into a den of lions by offering illegal prayers to God in front of an open window. The Book of Daniel tells the story, pointing out that Daniel "knelt down as usual in his upstairs room, with its windows open toward Jerusalem. He prayed three times a day, just as he had always done, giving thanks to his God."[2] This passage makes it clear that Daniel practiced a pattern of regular times of prayer that remained consistent no matter his circumstances. He was in good company, too!

The great Psalmist did the same, it would seem. Listen closely to the lyrics of this particular song from the Book of Psalms: "Morning, noon, and night I cry out in my distress, and the Lord hears my voice."[3] Though it is safe to assume that the Psalmist's prayers consisted of more than just moaning and groaning, it *is* good to know that the content of our prayers, be they praise or protest, seem to receive equal audience with God.

A quick flip through the Book of Psalms will confirm that the Psalmist moaned, groaned, and prayed to God regularly. Many of the songs in the Book of Psalms mention *morning prayers*—such as Psalm 5:3, 55:17, 59:16, 88:13, and 92:2—and many others mention *evening prayers*—such as Psalm 17:1–3, 42:8, 63:5–6, 119:55, and 141:2.

The songwriter of Psalm 65:8 even goes as far as to suggest that the morning and evening hours of prayer provide special access to God: "You make the gateways of the morning and the evening shout for joy."[4]

The Apostles must have been familiar with the ancient practice of fixed hours of prayer because they provide some of the clearest examples of the practice in the Book of Acts. For instance, the beginning of Acts notes that Peter and John went "up to the temple at the hour of prayer, at three o'clock in the

---

[2] Daniel 6:10.

[3] Psalm 55:17.

[4] NRSV.

afternoon."[5] And again, later in Acts, Peter prays again at the same hour: "One afternoon about three o'clock."[6] Six verses later, Peter has a life-changing experience when he interrupts a journey: "Peter went up on the flat roof to pray. It was about noon."[7]

Each of these note a specific time at which the prayers occurred. One occurs at noon (the sixth hour by Jewish reckoning) and the other two take place at three o'clock (the ninth hour). Prayer was so important to the Apostles and leaders of the Early Church that even prison incarceration could not keep them from prayer at a specific hour: "Around midnight Paul and Silas were praying and singing hymns to God, and the other prisoners were listening."[8]

The inclusion of the specific time at which the prayer was prayed is important. These are not random time stamps. Each of these verses offers clues into the prayer practices of our ancestors.

David and Daniel, Jesus and John, Peter and Paul—all seem to maintain fixed patterns of prayer in the daily practice of their faith. It is never presented as unusual, but instead, normative. The most devoted followers of God maintained regular, specific times of prayer.

Perhaps that is why it was said of the Early Church that it "devoted" itself to prayer.[9] Jesus had devoted himself to prayer and so did his followers. For them, prayer was one of the best—and dare I say, easiest—ways to follow in the footsteps of their Lord.

Few today find prayer easy, though.

---

[5]Acts 3:1, NRSV.

[6]Acts 10:3.

[7]Acts 10:9.

[8]Acts 16:25.

[9]Acts 1:14, 2:42, 6:4.

Prayer seems more like a chore, even a bore. If we pray at all, it is often little more than a short word offered over a quick meal or a rushed plea in a time of need. There rarely seems to be any time for regular times of prayer. Our busy lives crowd out the Creator, and we soon forget what the voice of God sounds like.

As I sat in the pew, I was certain that this was my story.

My busy life had crowded out my Creator. While I once thought that the distance I felt from God was the result of all the questions I had about my faith, the truth is that I had gotten busy—busy in the doing of ministry, but still, busy. Somewhere along the way I had lost the sound of God's voice.

I wondered if my spiritual breakdown would have ever occurred if I had engaged God intentionally through immovable hours of prayer. Perhaps my journey of deconstruction could not have been avoided, but if not, I am relatively certain that it would not have been so distressing had I maintained the rhythm of a regular spiritual practice such as prayer.

Perhaps I should cut myself a bit of slack though. And if you have difficulty with prayer, maybe you should as well. It is easy to fall into the trap of thinking that the mothers and fathers of the Early Church were super Christians, perfect and without fault. But we would be wrong to think that. They struggled in many of the same ways that we do, and faced similar difficulties to the ones we face today: busy lives, tough economic climates, and a great deal of cultural and social oppression.

One thing is quite clear from the historical record, though. When it came to prayer, early Christians avoided trying to *find* time and instead *made* time.

The Early Church ordered their life around their prayer schedule, rather than forcing their times of prayer into whatever time they had left after everything else was done.

It was important to early Christians to maintain regular times during which to pray. It doesn't seem to have been a "pray whenever you can" mentality. They prayed at specific times that coincided with the Jewish roots from which they had come: the third, sixth, and ninth hours.

The third hour (9:00 a.m.) coincided with the opening of the Temple and the first sacrifice of the day. The sixth hour (12:00 noon) was the main meal of the day. The ninth hour (3:00 p.m.) coincided with the final evening sacrifice and the closing of the Temple. It was customary to offer a blessing at each of these day's events, and it seems that many people in the Early Church prayed at these hours, no matter where they were or what they were doing.

One of the earliest documents that we have from the time period, *The Didache*, confirms that the Early Church often used these three ongoing times of prayer in their spiritual routine, and that the Lord's Prayer was the prayer to be prayed at these times.[10]

Lest we think that this was a limited practice among the most mature Christians, nearly every pastor, priest, and bishop in the Early Church wrote on the subject of prayer and strongly advocated for regular daily patterns of prayer.[11]

- Clement of Alexandria (c. 150–c. 215 CE), for example, mentions fixed hour prayer on the third, sixth, and ninth hours, but he encouraged his congregation to pray even more that just those three fixed hours.[12]
- Origen of Alexandria (c. 185–c. 254 CE) suggested that prayer "ought not to be performed less than three times

[10] *The Didache*, 8.3.

[11] If you want to go deeper into a study of Early Church prayer, look into the writings of Clement and Origen of Alexandria, Tertullian, Hippolytus, and Ignatius of Antioch.

[12] Clement, *Stromata,* 7.7,12.

each day ... and not even the time of night shall pass without such prayer, for David says, 'At midnight I rose to give thanks to you because of your righteous judgments.'" It seems Origen wanted his people to pray four times a day.[13]

While it's tough to say quite how it happened, it is clear by the 2nd century that much of the church in the West was praying according to regulated patterns of prayer:

- *Third, Sixth, and Ninth Hour Prayers:* These were continuations of the traditional Jewish hours of prayer followed by Jesus and the Apostles.
- *Morning and Evening Prayers:* These were connected to the sunrise and sunset as well as the Psalms of David. These were the most practiced of all the fixed-hour prayers, perhaps due in large part to their occurrence outside of the typical working day.
- *Night Prayers:* These had a very end-times focus that was linked with the hope and expectation of Jesus' return. Said Clement, "We must sleep in such a way that we might be easily awakened." A mid-slumber waking for prayer was seen to help accomplish this.[14]

By the dawn of the Middle Ages, the Early Church had crafted a very precise pattern of prayer in which nearly everyone participated. These were based on the practices of the psalmist who wrote: "I will praise you *seven times a day*," and, "I rise *at midnight* to thank you," for a total of eight periods of prayer each day.[15]

---

[13] Clement, *De Oratione,* 12.2.

[14] Clement, *Paed,* 2.9.

[15] Psalm 119:164a, 119:62a.

Saint Benedict's Eight Prayer Offices

Office	Time
Lauds	Sunrise
Prime	About 6:00 a.m.
Terce	Mid-morning
Sext	Noon
None	Mid-afternoon
Vespers	Sunset
Compline	Before retiring to bed
Vigils/Matins	Middle of the night

Adapted from: Jonathan Wilson-Hartgrove, *The Rule of Saint Benedict* (Brewster, MA: Paraclete Press, 2012), 39; and Kenneth V. Peterson, *Prayer as Night Falls: Experiencing Compline* (Brewster, MA: Paraclete Press, 2013), 18–19.

The early Christians believed that praying this way, eight times a day, brought them closest to fulfilling the Apostle Paul's directive to "pray without ceasing."[16]

The first Christians considered prayer such a key component of their spiritual lives that they began referring to their pattern of daily prayer as the "Divine Office" and the "Liturgy of the Hours." *Office* is a Latin word that means "task/duty" and *liturgy* is a Greek word with a similar meaning.

The early Christians saw their regular rhythms of prayer as a duty—a responsibility to which they felt it was necessary to commit themselves as wholly as possible.

Reconstructing Prayer

While the Early Church seemed to respond positively to the idea of a spiritual duty, modern Christians often tend to have a

[16] 1 Thessalonians 5:17, NRSV.

bit more difficulty with the idea of prayer being a duty. To see prayer—or any spiritual practice, for that matter—as a duty can be off-putting.

Over the years as a pastor, I began to notice that even the most dedicated followers of Jesus had a hard time wrapping their mind and heart around duty-oriented practices. We aren't big fans of doing something because we *have* to do it; we prefer to do something because we *want* to do it.

I didn't *want* to attend seven worship services a day at the Abbey. I was certain of that. I was less certain, though, what might happen if I did.

In crisis, it was the routine itself that drew me into the duty. I was in a place where I needed a consistent pattern to provide peace. So I plugged into the rhythms of the religious community and drank from the deep wells of the healing that the routine provided.

Over the course of my time at the Abbey, I spent a great deal of time contemplating and experiencing ancient rhythms. And each day, like clockwork, the monks and I gathered seven times a day for prayer.

An unexpected thing began to happen as I relinquished my personal preferences about prayer and participated in the Liturgy (duty) of the Hours of Prayer. I began to find comfort in the routine. And in the comfort, I began to sense the presence of God. My heart began to soften and my soul began to listen.

I was only at the Abbey for a week—less than seven days of seven liturgies a day—but the rhythm of the hours embedded itself in my spirit in ways that impacted me for months after my stay with the monks. Some of the prayer rhythms remained, even today.

Since the Abbey, I regularly find myself waking up in the middle of the night with an overwhelming feeling of the need to pray. During the day, often without thinking, I find myself pausing for prayer. Over the years, I have attached certain prayers to certain habits. Brushing my teeth, getting into the driver's seat of the car, arriving at the gym, opening my email, and other regular habits now have prayers tied to them. As I go through my daily routine, each habit is a reminder to pray for the person or problem I've committed to praying for during that practice.

The rhythm of the hours worked its way into my post-Abbey life in ways I hadn't expected, becoming the kindling for a reigniting of my faith. Although my prayer life was on life support when I arrived at the Abbey, the practice soon became as easy as breathing.

A regular routine of prayer became the mouth-to-mouth resuscitation to my soul.

Until my time at the Abbey, I had been of the opinion that prayer was best practiced in an off-the-cuff kind of way. My opinion had always been that the best prayers were the spontaneous kind (and when before a meal, preferably short). My whole life until this point had been one long experiment in *unforced* rhythms of prayer. I had been taught to believe that unforced, spontaneous prayers were a gift of freedom from stale, boring, ritualized prayers. But I was wrong.

I never considered the beauty and power in *forced* rhythms that use prayers written by others. There are prayers available to us that have been prayed for centuries or longer. We have access to prayers that have filled the spiritual wells of parched followers of Christ for generations. These prayers have stood the test of time and are still found to have value and give life. There is power in knowing that in the moments when my soul is dry, I can draw from the deep wells of others.

If I had missed the power of ancient prayer practices, I wondered what else I could have missed among the spiritual practices of the Early Church.

Reflect

1. What song, sacred or secular, best describes your prayer life?
2. Rate your current prayer life from 1–5 (with 5 being nearly perfect). Why did you rate yourself this way?
3. What other important questions does prayer help people answer?
4. Can you think of a time in your or your family's history when a prayer wasn't answered? If so, how does the story make you feel?
5. What is one thing you can do, no matter how small, to create a pattern of prayer in your life?

8 The Church Year

The greatest waste of time is the time that we spend trying to convince ourselves that we're not wasting it.

—Craig D. Lounsbrough,
certified professional life coach

"You have no idea."

The monk who had just uttered that line to me had gone glassy-eyed as his mind wandered to some unknown place.

Unknown to me, at least.

The question I had posed—"Do you ever get tired of the same rhythm every day?"—seemed simple to me.

The Trappist monks at the Abbey have taken a vow of lifetime commitment to their God, ongoing contemplation, and the rules of the Order. Within the enclosure of the Abbey, they will spend the rest of their days submitting to the rhythm of worship and prayer. And while the monks have all taken a vow of silence, they are still allowed to speak, in a limited way, when necessary.

Their seven daily hours of prayer require them to arrange the rest of their activities accordingly. It sounds like chaos to have so little flexibility, but I quickly sensed that it had the opposite effect. A strict rhythm of ordered living gave their lives unexpected stability, and I began to find myself longing for it.

"Do you ever get tired of the same rhythm every day?"

The monk had taken so long to answer that I thought I had breached protocol by asking him a question during an hour during which he was supposed to remain silent. But just as I was ready to apologize and uncomfortably extract myself from the situation, he looked back at me, responding:

"No … and yes."

He must have seen the obvious confusion on my face over his nonanswer answer. He breathed deeply, pausing for an uncomfortably long moment.

"The routine is as natural as breathing; I don't think about it much anymore. I simply shape my life by it and it brings me," he paused again "… Christ."

I had expected him to say *comfort.*

I had expected him to say *peace.*

I had NOT expected him to say *Christ.*

By the look on his face, I think he expected a different word to come out as well.

The monks of the Abbey practice a rhythm that is nearly as old as Christianity itself; as I had learned, their gatherings for worship are timed to an ancient rhythm that is modeled after the prayer patterns of Jesus, the Apostles, and Judaism.

In the years after the Advent of Jesus and before the advent of the Bible, Christians leveraged the power of routines and rhythms to form deep faith, and the monks at the Abbey follow those basic rhythms each day … forever.

They set their lives by the rhythmic pace of the calendar of the Abbey.

As much as I wanted to see the monks' schedule of round-the-clock worship, work, and contemplation as utter insanity, it would have required me to ignore the fact that I too was locked into an utterly insane schedule that attempted to juggle a dizzying array of commitments, classes, breaks, conferences, activities, and expectations. Add in the seasons, celebrations, religious observances, and holidays, and the resulting behemoth of a calendar I try to navigate looks far more overwhelming than the simple ebb and flow of the monks' endless seven-worship daily liturgy.

Like the monks, we all set our lives by time. The calendar is the greatest rhythmic force in most people's lives, and if you are like me, the incessant chaos of the calendar feels like a strait-jacket that keeps you from peace rather than being a tool that brings it.

It wasn't until I experienced a different ordering of time—and the resulting feeling of freedom from disorder—that I began to ask whether I really wanted order to be my life, or for my life to be in order.

I had certainly felt the tension of competing calendars over the years. Like most people, I had to wrestle with difficult questions like, "Do I let the kids play sports on Sunday mornings?" or "Should family and work commitments come before church activities and events?" or "Should we attend Sunday morning services when it falls on vacation, July Fourth, or most of all,

Christmas morning?" While the family always somehow found a way to put everything in order, there was always a growing and uncomfortable tension between my religious commitments and regular life.

Theologian James K. A. Smith points to the problem when he flatly states what we all intuitively already know: "Christians are a people whose year does not simply map onto the calendar of the dominant culture."[1]

The Early Church Calendar

Early Christians believed that the Christian faith was meant to be countercultural.[2] But rather than see Christianity as a cudgel to antagonize culture—much like we see in the church today—the Early Church only desired to create and protect its own beautiful new culture around its first love, Jesus. Early Christians saw their interaction with time as an opportunity to align themselves more closely to what, in their minds, was a countercultural Kingdom of God.

The Early Church sought to sanctify time itself.

It should come as little surprise that the first countercultural Christian event to be regularly celebrated was Sunday itself. Christians set aside Sunday almost immediately as an ongoing celebration of the "Lord's Day" in commemoration of Christ's Resurrection. It is difficult to underestimate how radical an adjustment it was to shift from Friday/Saturday to Sunday as the primary day of worship.

By the end of the 2nd century, Wednesdays and Fridays had been added to the calendar as additional sacred days set aside for

---

[1] James K. A. Smith, *Desiring the Kingdom: Worship, Worldview, and Cultural Formation, vol. 1, Cultural Liturgies* (Grand Rapids, MI: Baker Academic, 2009), 156.
[2] See John 17:14–17; Romans 12:2; 2 Corinthians 6:14, 17; Colossians 2:8; Jam. 1:27; and 1 John 2:15.

fasting. And while fasting may not seem celebratory, the act of replacing plates of food with times of prayer was a powerful statement of their commitment to intentionally create religious rhythms that were in conflict with their normal daily routines. Setting aside time to fast and pray appealed to their desire to sanctify time ... and thus, themselves.

Though each Sunday was a celebration of the Resurrection, the Early Church wanted to go further, so it began setting aside a single Sunday a year, Easter, for a major remembrance of it. But there was so much to celebrate that a day wasn't enough. Eventually, the entire week leading up to Easter Sunday was set aside as an annual opportunity to remember Jesus' journey through death to resurrection. All of the rites, fasts, and feasts of the week culminated in the Great Triduum of Holy Thursday, Good Friday, and Holy Saturday.[3]

By the 4th century, the sanctification of time through countercultural religious calendaring was firmly entrenched in the church's yearly rhythms. The Early Church had greatly expanded Holy Week to include Lent as a time of pre-Easter preparation, and Pentecost was added as a post-Easter celebration marking the coming of the Holy Spirit and founding of the church.

Soon, the calendar included the season of Christmas, a celebration of Christ's birth, and Epiphany, to honor the arrival of the Magi from the East and to commemorate Christ's later baptism. And while Advent is the traditional start of the Christian calendar (not January 1), it was the last season to be added to it.

The Modern-Day Liturgical Cycle

The Early Church's desire to mark time by making an annual pilgrimage through the most important milestones of Jesus' life

---

[3]A *Triduum* is a period of three days of prayer before a feast, such as Easter.

became a remarkably effective tool for faith formation that invited people into a year-long journey that began with anticipation at Advent, journeyed through Epiphany, reflected at Lent, celebrated at Easter, and remembered its roots at Pentecost.

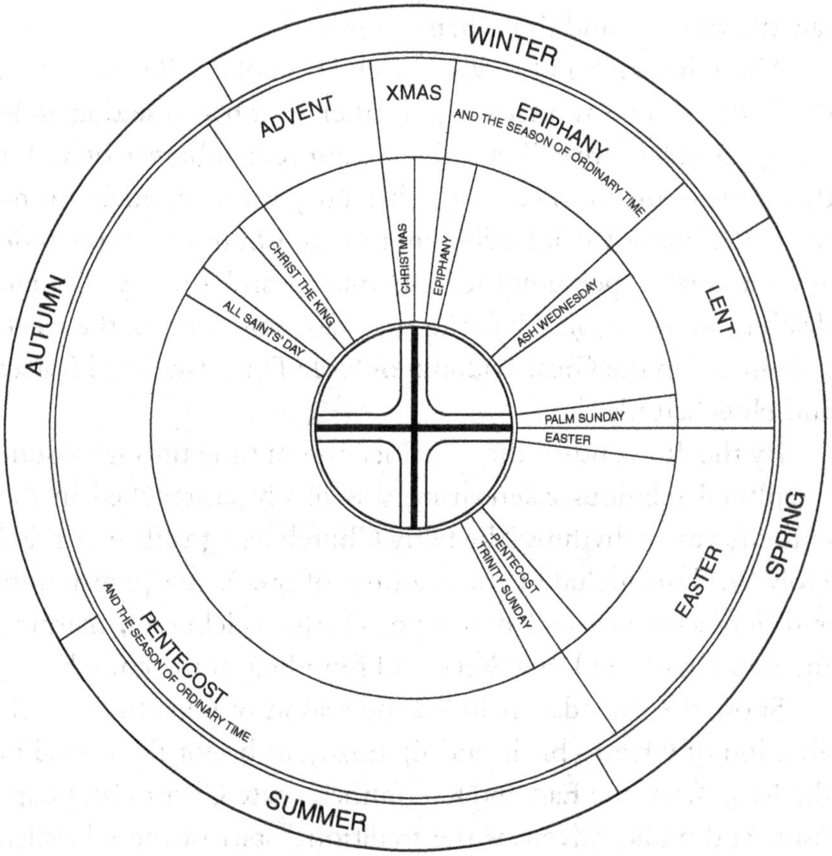

Source: Sacred Ordinary Days / https://sacredordinarydays.com/blogs/news/formation-foundations-2-get-to-know-liturgical-year / last accessed January 18, 2024.

This unique calendar, developed over centuries during some of the most harrowing days the church has ever witnessed, still stands as its single greatest formational achievement. It remains relatively unchanged since the time the Early Church developed it, not by decision or decree, but organically over a lengthy period of time, from various places and people. The word *liturgy* itself comes from the Greek words *lēitos* (public) and *ergos* (working), meaning "the work of the people."

The *Liturgical Cycle*—sometimes called the *Church Calendar*, *Christian Cycle*, or *The Church Year*—was a Christ-centered clock that set out to imprint a different rhythm of seasons, celebrations, and sacred days in opposition of secular rhythms and celebrations. This annual cycle proved to be so effective that it firmly established the Early Church as a countercultural group; so revolutionary was it that many early Christians considered the act of following the Liturgical Cycle to be an act of civil disobedience.

Even though the church has used some or all of the Liturgical Calendar for nearly the entirety of its history, using the Liturgical Calendar can still feel like civil disobedience in many Christian contexts today.

It did for me.

I was taught to mark and avoid anything and everything liturgical, and I was raised to believe that "the work of the people" was a tool of the devil. "These things are going to take you away from Jesus," I was told. But as I began to dip my toe into deeper waters, I was surprised to find life in the church's oldest countercultural rhythms.

Before the Abbey, the extent of my participation in the Liturgical Calendar ended at Christmas and Easter. But even then, early Christians would have been shocked at how anemic my celebrations of these events were. They wouldn't have understood why I only spent a day celebrating Christmas and then tearing down the decorations and moving on. They would have been aghast at the thought of relegating the resurrection festivities to a single Sunday. These were seasons, not single days.

I'm terribly embarrassed to admit that I didn't know that "The Twelve Days of Christmas" wasn't just a song but a period of time—12 days, go figure—when the church celebrated the arrival of the Savior in Bethlehem. For 12 full days, the entire church celebrated the arrival of Jesus, the promised Messiah, in Bethlehem. And the celebration was as lively on the twelfth day as it was on December 25.

For me, the mirth and cheer of Christmas came in the days before the 25th of December, but the Early Church did the exact opposite, spending the days before Christmas in intentional solemnity. This period of time is the season it called Advent, and I found that there *is* a very big difference between Christmas and Advent. Advent was the annual opportunity to experience the longing of waiting for the Savior to arrive, much like all of humanity waited and longed for the Messiah to come before Bethlehem. Because early Christians didn't want to rush right to the celebration, they spent Advent in solemnity, waiting until the Christmas Eve Vigil to begin their 12-day celebration.

Easter was much the same way; more shock and awe for me. While I celebrated Easter with a full day devoted to Jesus, early Christians spent weeks—50 days, to be exact—celebrating a season that came to be called Eastertide. The resurrection was so important to them that a single day could not contain it. And like Christmas' season of preparation (Advent), Easter had a season of preparation as well: Lent. I also had avoided Lent because … this won't shock you … it was too Catholic.

Eating fish on Fridays and giving up chocolate was considered so sinful in the religious context in which I grew up that participating in Lent would have been as bad as dancing or playing card games, which is to say, it would be the worst sin imaginable to participate in. But a quick look at the roots of Lent show that it was and is grounded in an intentional preparation of the community of faith in anticipation of Easter. It is about getting one's self ready.

What could possibly be the problem with preparing my heart? I wondered.

The more I learned about the calendar of the Early Church and its liturgies of celebration, the more embarrassed I became at my audacity of having ever thought that my anemic Evangelical celebrations were the better way ... or way better, for that matter. I had scoffed at Roman Catholics and other Christians who chose to implement a year-long calendar of celebrations and events that set their hearts and lives in time with the story of redemption brought by Jesus, but I had been wrong. I wondered how I could have ever thought that my Evangelical church's annual routine of holy days and holidays—Mother's Day, Memorial Day, Father's Day, the Fourth of July, Veterans Day, Thanksgiving, Christmas, Valentine's Day, Good Friday, and Easter—could have been seen as more sacred, let alone helpful, as the calendar that the church has used to mark time—and embed Christ into the hearts and lives of Christians—for nearly 2,000 years.

I didn't know that Epiphany, which begins on January 6, also often included a "Twelfth Night" celebration on January 5. The church traditionally held that the Magi arrived from the East on this night, so they would celebrate the end of Christmastide—and its 12 days of merrymaking—with the giving of gifts. Epiphany, rather than Christmas, was the traditional day of gift-giving in the church.

I didn't know that Halloween is a contraction of All Hallows' Eve, which, like Christmas Eve, is an important day of preparation before a major religious holiday. In the case of Halloween, it is a preparation day for All Saints' Day, or its original name, All Hallows' Day ("Hallows," from the word *hallow*, which is an old word for "holy" or "honor"). You might recognize it from the second line of the Lord's Prayer, "Our Father who is in Heaven, *hallowed* be your name. ..." When the church began to celebrate all Christians who have passed, we were given All Hallows'/Souls'/Saints' Day, which gave us All Hallows' Eve.

I wondered if this information would have put my parents at ease about letting my sister and me trick-or-treat.

It's a religious holiday, mom!

There are many reasons why the average Christian might avoid using the Liturgical Calendar as a tool to shape their lives around, but hard feelings from 500 years ago are probably at the root of most of them. Despite popular opinion in some quarters of Protestantism, the Reformation did more to divide the church than it did to protect good doctrine.

The Great Reformation divided the church from itself, yes. But even worse, it divided the church from some of its most life-giving tools. Tools that have been refined over a period of 1,500 years shouldn't be so easily dismissed.

Once I realized that all of these tools were developed when the church was united—no division between Catholic and Protestant, East and West—it gave me the permission I needed to explore these ancient spiritual practices for my own formation.

Reconstructing the Church Year

In the days, months, and eventually, years after my time at the Abbey, I began to (re)orient my life to the calendar of the Early Church, almost without thinking. It was the natural progression of my somewhat anemic celebrations of Christmas and Easter. But there was so much life and growth, and I had been missing out.

That first Christmas after the Abbey, I dipped my toes into Advent. I discovered an entire library full of music that the church had developed for this season of anticipation and waiting. I had often avoided these songs because I had deemed them too solemn for December. But now it made sense, and these songs resonated in places of my soul that had never been allowed to long for, sit sad, or cry out to God. I rediscovered the power of "Come Thou Long Expected Jesus" and "O Come, O Come, Emmanuel." These songs replaced "Joy to the World" in my playlist, which I saved until Christmas Day and thereafter.

I purchased an Advent Wreath for our family table, and we lit one new candle each week at dinnertime. I began teaching my children about Advent, and each night, we talked about what it must have been like to have to wait on Jesus to arrive. The first week we lit the *hope* candle and reflected on what it was like to hope for something that never seemed to come. The second week we lit the *peace* candle; the third week, the *joy* candle; and the *love* candle the fourth week. By the time we finally lit the tall white candle (the Christ Candle) in the center of the wreath at sunset on Christmas Eve, my kids had spent a month talking about the power of the coming Christ. They were ready to celebrate the true meaning of Christmas.

I began sending our Christmas Cards after Christmas Day, during the 12-day Christmastide rather than during Advent. And they always feature the Magi. I refused to take down the Christmas tree until January 5—the twelfth and final night of Christmas—no matter how dead it was, and we bought and ate our first King Cake of Epiphany, a traditional dessert that celebrates the Magi and is filled with symbols of the religious season. Yes, we used a large cake as a tool to teach our children—and let's be honest, ourselves—the developing story of redemption.

For Lent, I began giving up something that was a true sacrifice for the 40 days before Easter. But I didn't just give something up, I took on things during that time to draw closer to Christ. One year, I journaled. Another year, I took a picture a day of something that reminded me of God. Once, I read through the Gospel of Mark.

On Pentecost, we had cake and a birthday celebration for the Early Church. Pentecost, of course, is the day when the church was birthed, according to Acts 2. Our cake wished a "Happy 1,985th Birthday" to the church.

On All Saints' Day, I spent time reflecting on those "saints" in my life who had brought me closer to Jesus, but who were now in his presence.

These rhythms began to embed themselves into my life, and then they began to impact my family calendar. The rhythms weren't stale in the least; they gave me the opportunity to use creativity to teach my kids, and all of these longstanding celebrations of the church become a source of life for all of us. I began to notice the power and beauty of these ancient rhythms and how the ancient Liturgical Calendar asked me to set aside lesser stories to participate in a grander one.

The historic Church Calendar asks me to aside the lesser stories—patriotic holidays, Hallmark holidays, and even my own events—to participate fully in a more important one. To align my rhythms with the Church Calendar, I had to begin to extricate myself from other things and other thinking.

Along the way, I discovered that the liturgy is a heart, mind, and body strategy for faith formation that puts our whole lives through a regimen of repeated practices to get hold of our soul, and, like a compass, orient them toward the Kingdom of God. Rather than the Liturgical Cycle being a rote routine that was little more than mindless followership—as I had been raised to believe—it, instead, became a force for change in my life that often exceeded the transformational power of the Bible.

"Do you ever get tired of the same rhythm every day?" I had asked the monk.

"No … and yes," he had said.

"… The routine is as natural as breathing; I don't think about it much anymore. I simply shape my life by it and it brings me … Christ."

He had given me the *no* part of his "no and yes" answer, but I was most interested in the "*yes*."

"But what about the 'Yes' part?" I asked, pressing him beyond where I think he wanted to go.

A slight smile crossed his face, and he got a distant look in his eye.

"We never change chairs," he said, pointing back behind himself to the sanctuary within the Abbey. "Your chair is your chair … for life. We spend worship chanting psalms. All day, all night, every day. Forever."

He paused, clearly wondering whether he should continue.

"The brother who sits directly behind me sings rather loudly. He has a strong voice. But worse than the level of his volume is his timing. He is always a half-beat behind the rhythm. All day, all night, every day. Off rhythm. Forever."

He paused.

"I'm learning humility … slowly."

In the years since I was at the Abbey, I've gotten increasingly better at shaping my life around rhythms that lead to redemption and hope, rather than away from it. But I've also had to forgive myself in those moments when I've been a half-beat behind.

The point is progress, not perfection. And in all things, humility.

Reflect

1. What is your favorite holiday or season? What was it as a child?
2. Do you have a healthy or unhealthy relationship with time and the calendar?
3. The Early Church sought to sanctify time. What are some ways that you might do that in your life?
4. Do you have any holiday traditions/rhythms that are toxic or counterproductive?
5. What is at least one tradition from this chapter that you would like to implement in your own context?

9 The Saints

For me to be a saint means to be myself.
—Thomas Merton

One is unable to sneeze in the Abbey without having to say "Excuse me" to a painting of some saint or a statue of the Virgin Mary. Being surrounded by so many icons may have brought some people peace, but for me, they were simply another reason to feel disconnected from the spiritual roots of the Abbey.

My awkward and uneasy relationship with the saints is due, in large part, to my post-Reformation upbringing. Just like every child eventually reaches the age where they leave belief in Santa behind, Protestants left behind belief in saints somewhere circa 1500 CE.

Every time I apologize to a saint in the Abbey, I imagine that somewhere in central Indiana, my grandfather is rolling over in his grave.

Though my grandfather loathed the idea of saints, he loved the idea of Santa Claus. He considered both Santa and the saints as characters of make-believe, but he loved Christmas so much that he gave Santa Claus the grace that he could never find for the saints. A bit like Ebenezer Scrooge after his redemption, my grandfather was famous for knowing how to keep Christmas alive and well, if any man alive possessed the knowledge. Grandpa loved the sights, sounds, smells, food, and especially the gifts of Christmas. Most of my pictures of Grandpa are from annual family gatherings on Christmas morning. In every picture, I am right beside him; we were inseparable in life and in photo. And in every picture we are wearing huge smiles … and flannel.

As close as my grandfather and I were, I don't think that he would have ever understood my time at the Abbey or my need to explore the ancient roots of my faith. I also don't believe that he would have understood my faith crisis or all of the questions that were driving it.

Faith came easily for him, as it does for some.

I am also quite certain that my grandfather never noticed the hypocrisy of his love for Santa Claus and his loathing of the saints.

There is a very real person behind the legend of Santa Claus, and his name is Nicholas of Myra, Asia Minor (modern-day Turkey). Born in the 3rd century, Nicholas's early years were a roller coaster. While he had the good fortune of being born into a very wealthy family who were followers of Jesus, he had the bad fortune of losing those parents in an epidemic when he was still very young. But as often happens, children who are guided well by their parents at a young age tend to continue on those paths later in life.

Nicholas grew up holding strong to his faith and loosely to his purse strings, giving away all of his wealth. The poor, sick, and under-resourced became the recipients of his financial fortune, while Nicholas devoted himself even more fully to the faith of his father and mother.

Entering the priesthood, Nicholas eventually became the Bishop of Myra, an extremely prestigious pastoral position that he leveraged to further serve others. Church history nerds will be fascinated to know that Nicholas was even a delegate to one of the most famous (if not *the* most famous) and important meetings in church history, the Council of Nicaea in 325 CE.[1] (Bonus points if you knew that there is an old story that says Nicholas became so heated over the heresy he was hearing at the Council, that he slapped [or punched] the offender ... forever giving new meaning to the phrase: "He's making a list and checking it twice, he's going to find out who's naughty or nice!")

Though the centuries after Nicholas's death have added a number of stories and legends—many questionable in their veracity—to the man who would eventually be recognized by the church as Saint Nicholas, none of these stories ever quite upstage the amazing true story. Flying reindeer with nasal abnormalities aside, Saint Nicholas continues to inspire children and children-at-heart to be a little less selfish and a lot more generous to those in need. Each year on December 25, much of the world celebrates the legacy of a man who is not a myth, but a legendary member of the clergy worth remembering.

While the world remembers Saint Nicholas the Legend (or Santa Claus as many call his alter ego) on December 25, many churches around the world celebrate Saint Nicholas the Bishop on the anniversary of his death, December 6. In Europe, for example, many Christians give their Christmas presents on December 6, Saint Nicholas Day, allowing Christmas Day to be a celebration fully focused on the birth of Christ.

---

[1] While the Council took up consideration of many issues that were facing the church at the time, the topic of Arianism was its most pressing problem: was Jesus truly divine or was he only a created being?

Growing up, Saint Nicholas was a "safe saint." My grandfather and the rest of the family looked the other way and let us celebrate Santa. But Santa is not the only saint celebrated by those who otherwise ignore these ancient Christian role models.

The Deeper Meaning of the Saints

Saint Patrick's Day celebrates a saint of the church. Patrick was a 5th-century Christian missionary and bishop known for being the Apostle of Ireland. Patrick's story is riveting, and it deserves far more time in the retelling than in the drinking every March 17. And, as with Nicholas, Saint Patrick's Day is celebrated on the day of his death.

There is also Valentine, a saint of the church who has his day every 14th of February. Valentine was a member of the clergy who ministered to persecuted Christians. Though the story of how his name became associated with love is quite complicated—and downright gruesome, to be honest—the truth of his life of faith and death as a martyr is decidedly uncomplicated. In 269 CE, Valentine was sentenced to a three-part execution of a beating, stoning, and decapitation. He was eventually named a saint by the church, and if you were wondering, yes, we celebrate Saint Valentine on the anniversary of his death, February 14th.

When we celebrate Santa Claus, Saint Patrick's Day, and Valentine's Day, we are participating in a long-standing tradition of remembering saints of the church, but we are often blissfully unaware of the significance of the celebrations because we see them as secular rather than sacred.

As I began to learn about some of these saints, I was saddened that many otherwise upstanding Christians, like my grandfather, resisted considering the value of these saints of the church. Wouldn't it better to connect Valentine's Day to the story of a saint rather than roses and boxes of chocolates? Many in the church seem to have forgotten—or never encountered—the religious significance of Santa Claus, shamrocks, and Cupid.

Origins of Sainthood

There are very few topics, ancient or modern, that have drawn as much ire as that of the saints. Even the Early Church had some difficulty understanding the need for a group of next-level Christians like the saints. They seemed elite, untouchable, and counterproductive to some. From the church's earliest days, the topic of the saints caused sharp disagreements between many bishops and their congregations.

Nearly 1,500 years later, the topic of saints would divide the Protestant reformers from the Roman Catholic Church, and it continues to be deeply divisive between many segments of the church even today. If the topic weren't already complicated enough, the various ways in which the church has used the word *saint* over the years makes it all the more confusing.

We should be gentle with those who aren't ready to accept the saints. The topic can be confusing, and we must admit that we see this confusion taking shape even as early as the New Testament period. And, yes, the Bible *does* discuss the saints several times … positively.

Shocking to some, I know.

The Bible tells us that the first saints of the church were all of its members, not just a select group. That is important, of course. Notice how the Apostle Paul begins his letter to the church in Rome: "To all God's beloved in Rome, who are called to be saints … ."[2] When Paul later writes to the church in the city of Corinth, he addresses his letter "to those who are

[2] Romans 1:7, NRSV.

sanctified in Christ Jesus, called to be saints . . ."[3] It is clear from this and other uses of the Greek word *hagiois* (saints) that all of the followers of The Way were considered saints—that is, holy and set apart.

Yet even in those early days when the New Testament was still unfolding in real time, there seems to have been a special group of individuals—in addition to elders and deacons—who were set apart from the larger body of believers and were called "the saints." In the Book of Acts, for instance, Luke writes about a time when there was a need for "calling the saints and widows" in order to witness the raising of Tabitha from the dead.[4]

After the passing of the last Apostles, the idea of a separate and set-apart group of Christ followers—referred to simply as "the saints"—continued to grow in popularity among the early believers. To understand the draw they felt to create a subgroup of more spiritually mature members, we have to better understand the Greco-Roman world in which they lived.

Both Greek and Roman cultures had a long-standing tradition of celebrating the passing of loved ones on the anniversary of their death, usually with a special meal at the site of their burial. Families would come together and picnic at the tomb, share stories, and remember the life of their beloved. These annual gatherings with the deceased served to both honor the departed and keep their memory alive. Many Christ followers would have participated in these funerary meals before coming to faith as they were a normal and expected part of the fabric of social culture, and many new Christians would have seen no conflict between their new faith and the continuation of memorializing departed family members.

---

[3] 1 Corinthians 1:2, NRSV.

[4] Acts 9:41, NRSV.

Since the beginning of Christianity, there has been an uneasy relationship between Christians and the culture around them.

Growing up, I had been taught to focus on the tension between the outside culture in which I lived and the church culture. There was no attempt to reconcile our faith with rhythms and practices of the culture. I always saw my role to be antagonistic with the world around me.

For early Christians, though, it wasn't so easy. Christianity was still being formed, and an influx of "pagan" belief into the church left a sometimes messy orthodoxy in its wake. The early Christians had to decide whether to:

- Avoid participation in secular practices completely.
- Continue their secular cultural practices without much care as to how it affected their faith.
- Reimagine their secular cultural practices to fit their unique and newfound identity in Christ.

While many modern Christians tend to feel most comfortable choosing between the first two options, early Christians most often chose the third. They tended to avoid completely distancing themselves from their surrounding culture as much as they avoided ignoring its effects. Early believers regularly sought creative ways to unite faith and culture, choosing instead to transform long-standing secularized practices into new, rethought Christ-centered ones. These new Christ-centered takes on old cultural ones ended up infusing life and energy into the church.

In the long run, the co-opting and infusion of cultural practices into Christianity often ended up overtaking the secular practice altogether.

For example, Polycarp was a bishop of the church and something of a celebrity in 155 CE. He had been a disciple of the

Apostle John—yes, *that* John—and was ordained as the Bishop of Smyrna by *that* John. When the early persecution of Christians began to intensify, key figures like Polycarp were targeted because of their power and prominence. When Polycarp refused to burn incense to the Emperor of Rome, he was burned alive at the stake and then stabbed to death when the fire would not kill him. A written account picks up the story from there:

> *And so we afterwards took up his bones which are more valuable than precious stones and finer than refined gold, and laid them in a suitable place; where the Lord will permit us to gather ourselves together, as we are able, in gladness and joy, and to celebrate the birthday of his martyrdom for the commemoration of those that have already fought in the contest, and for the training and preparation of those that shall do so hereafter.*[5]

In death, Polycarp became a more important example than he had ever been in his life.

The Early Church thought of Polycarp and other martyrs' deaths as the perfect opportunity to celebrate the hero's birth into the presence of God, the hope of every Christian … especially those facing persecution. As such, the Christians began celebrating "birthdays" on the anniversary of martyrs like Polycarp's death, their death being the day of their birth into Jesus' arms. Christians under intense persecution looked to these martyrs for strength and courage; they were thankful to have examples of unwavering faith under fire.

As the list of martyrs grew longer, the Early Church so revered their example that it began to think of those who willingly sacrificed their lives for the faith as a group of believers

[5] *The Martyrdom of Polycarp*, 18.2-3.

who were set apart and deserving of consideration as a worthy example to be followed by all. Their example became so important that the Early Church began adding their remembrance meals to local church calendars, encouraging the faithful to celebrate their "Birth Days" and remember the extraordinary example of their lives.

Sainthood as Honoring the Faithful

Fast-forward to today, and depending on how you count them, there are a lot of saints. The Roman Catholic Church officially lists more than 10,000 saints. That means there are somewhere in the neighborhood of 10,000 examples of people who had a faith story that was considered worth remembering. It also means that there are also around 10,000 Christ-followers whose lives of faith my grandfather would have discounted simply for having the audacity to be considered a saint.

But we should correct the record just a bit for my grandfather and others. What was going on in the Early Church was *not* worship of the saints at all. The Church Fathers and early theologians insisted that God alone was to be worshipped, and the church fiercely protected Jesus as being God, not us. But the Early Church also saw value in honoring faithful followers of Jesus. Just as we might ask someone to pray on our behalf today, the early Christians continued to ask saints to intercede for them in death. But why?

The Early Church saw the boundary between this life and the next less like a thick, impenetrable door and more like a partially obscured window. Since departed saints were thought to be in the immediate presence of God, they were thus in an equal or better position than still-alive Christians to advocate to God on their behalf. To them, the veil between this life and the next was so thin as to be barely present.

Sadly, the origin and ongoing place of the saints within Christianity has been largely misunderstood, especially among Evangelicals. Even today, Catholics and Protestants are largely in agreement on the value of saints for the church. The Common Catechism—created by representatives of both faith traditions—says of the saints:

> *The main intention of the veneration of the saints is to glorify God's grace in real men and women as they exist in historical time. Veneration of the saints is not adoration of the saints, but celebration of them as witnesses to the triumphant grace of God and as models for the Christian life.*[6]

The Common Catechism provides balance, something desperately needed in Christian conversations today, and it allows us to see how our church ancestors used the idea of saints as worthy examples of the faith for young followers of Christ.

Saints as Role Models

Every parent understands the importance of finding good role models for their children, but it is often easier said than done. It is easily forgotten that the importance of good role models never really goes away. As the problems in life become more complex, so does the need to have help from others who have walked similar paths before us. When faced with the need for a reliable source of examples for our children or ourselves, many turn to the Bible, assuming that there is no better benchmark for life than the Good Book itself.

And while the Bible *is* an unparalleled resource for helping humanity know God, the problem with using the Bible as a

---

[6] Feiner, Johannes, and Lukas Vischer, *The Common Catechism: A Book of Christian Faith* (New York: Seabury Press, 1975).

primary role model and decision-maker in life is that it wasn't designed for that purpose. Encouraging others to take every question and concern to the pages of the Bible may ultimately prove counterproductive. Every choice in life cannot be clearly arbitrated by Scripture. Doing so creates a Paper Pope and places authority in a book rather than the person of Jesus as originally intended.

The Bible *does* help us know Jesus better, of course, but it is *not* the only way that we can better know and understand Jesus. Much to the surprise of my grandfather, who believed that the Bible is sufficient for everything and nothing else is sufficient for anything, there are sometimes better ways than the Bible to learn about God.

One of the best examples of this reality is the Apostle Paul who, in a letter to the church community in Corinth, famously encourages those who are spiritually weak to look to his own example, saying, "Imitate me as I imitate Christ."[7] Paul says, in effect, "I am going to be following Jesus, so you may follow me and do as I do." In so doing, Paul gives all of us permission to find and follow real-world examples of Christ-likeness whenever we have difficulty relating to the sometimes two-dimensional characters of Scripture.

Real-world role models who exhibit dynamic faith in Christ are dramatically important for faith formation. Knowing that there are others out there like us helps us to see that we are not alone in this world. When our hearts are connected with someone or something beyond ourselves, we no longer feel isolated or separated from others—a feeling that is prevalent in the world despite our connectedness through cell phones and social media. When we see that we are connected to a grander story, we experience hope and a sense that our value is greater than we may have first imagined it could be.

---

[7] 1 Corinthians 4:16, 11:1.

When we feel spiritually connected to Christ through others, we are able to see more than just vibrant examples of faith in action; we are given the capacity to imagine a future where we too could become a person of such vibrant faith that we would be worthy of being imitated, like the saints.

There is power in believing that we could be someone else's saint.

And that is the difficulty with the celebration of the saints. There is an obvious disconnect that comes in trying to connect with the stories of ancient saints of 1,500 years or so ago. It's hard to blame anyone—teenager or otherwise—for having trouble relating to the stories of Patrick or Polycarp.

Ancient saints and their struggles rarely seem very relevant today, and I wasn't sure that could easily be changed as I looked around the Abbey at all of the stuffy examples of studious living that were ensconced in paintings with halos and hand gestures.

The sound of the chanting monks bounces its way around the Abbey. The reverberation would be most pleasant, were it not for the one or two who were a bit off-key. A few tonally challenged monks, though, are not enough to distract someone who, like me, has been sitting in congregational singing environments since diapers.

My grandfather had a love for singing. Sadly, he neither possessed the ability to sing on key nor the lovely voice by which to do it. Yet, what grandpa lacked in tonality he more than made up for in volume. Each and every Sunday he and my grandmother could be found in their regular seats, five rows in front of my own, and each and every Sunday I could count on hearing my grandfather's bellowing just above the choir … and just below the melody.

The most important thing I remember about my grandfather isn't his less-than-stellar singing voice, but that he was in his seat every single service to prove it. Even when he should have been home for reasons of weather or health, he was there.

He was *always* there. My grandfather's love for Christmas was exceeded only by his love for Jesus. He was more than just the patriarch of our family of misfits—of which I was chief among them—he was a spiritual lighthouse, brightly showing the way home for any family member who had become lost on the rough seas of life. He was the type of Christian that every person in the church loved, respected, and looked to as a great example of faith in action.

There were many boring sermons where I would pass the time staring at his head of brilliant white hair and hoping that I would someday inherit the beauty of his hair and the strength of his faith. Having long ago lost the battle to keep the hair, I am now locked in the fight of my life to keep the other.

I wonder if Grandpa might be the key to keeping it?

Looking around the Abbey, I see many monks whom I imagine are wonderful examples of faith in action. I assume that each of them have their own riveting stories of transformation, but their faith seems as inaccessible to me as the saints of old. These monks are people whom I have come to respect, but they are not people who I *know*. Their stories are powerful, I am certain, but none could ever be as powerful to me as the story of a faithful grandfather whose DNA I am blessed to carry.

As I sit with that thought and begin to reflect on my life, I realize that there are many other individuals throughout my story who have lived lives of deep faith, experienced the miraculous moving of God on their behalf, and whose stories are well known to me. They, like my grandfather, lived lives of amazing faith, experienced miraculous moments, and maintained tremendous character and integrity. These family saints include my father-in-law, an old professor, a longtime pastor, a friend who I've known longer than a lifetime, my wife, and a handful of others.

One of my grandfather's favorite hymns—judging by the most important musical metric: how loudly he sang it—was the first hymn in the hymnal, Hymn 001, "Come Thou Fount of Every Blessing." In the hymn, there is a line in the second verse that my grandfather always seemed to sing with an extra special level of gusto:

Here I raise my Ebenezer; Hither by Thy help I'm come. …

As a young boy, I used to imagine the song leader lifting Scrooge off the ground in response to that line, which is to say, I had absolutely no idea what it meant. But I now understand that the hymn writer was co-opting an image from the Hebrew Scriptures. In 1 Samuel, the prophet "took a stone and set it up … and named it Ebenezer; for he said, 'Thus far the Lord has helped us.'"[8]

Ebenezer is an ancient Hebrew word that means "stone of help." In the passage, Samuel lifts up a stone as a symbol of God's help, a memorial.

And it was as if, in that moment of discovery, all of the pieces fell into place. My grandfather belted that line because he was

[8] 1 Samuel 7:12.

remembering all of the times where God had helped him. Each opportunity to sing the line was a reminder to him of God's presence along the ups and downs of life. I was blessed to know about many of those moments because I knew my grandfather well … and because he wasn't stingy with his God stories.

Sitting there in the Abbey, I realized that I have not been as giving to my children.

Do they know my stories?

Do they know my grandfather's stories?

Do I tell them of my family's Ebenezers?

For me, my grandfather himself is an Ebenezer, a person in my faith journey that is a symbol of God's presence, goodness, and grace.

My grandfather is a saint in the truest and deepest sense of the word.

Reconstructing Saints

In the years since my time at the Abbey, I have begun to collect the names and stories of the saints in my own life, and I regularly return to them when I begin to lose sight of Jesus. Their stories never fail to point me back to him. Some are relatives, some are friends, and some are icons of the faith.

I began writing down these stories and sharing them with my children over dinner. Once we cooked my grandfather's favorite meal—homemade chicken and dumplings from his hometown in the hollers of Kentucky—and I told stories about his faith to my children while they ate his favorite food.

My son carries my grandfather's name as a reminder of his legacy. My other son carries the name of my wife's grandfather, another man of deep faith. My daughter carries the name of my mother and my wife's mother, both saints in our respective lives.

When we celebrate Saint Nicholas Day, Valentine's Day, and Saint Patrick's Day, we make sure to tell the stories of these saints. Even Martin Luther King, Jr. Day gives us a chance to talk about a modern hero of faith, and we sometimes serve his favorite dish, fried chicken, as any Southerner should be able to cook well.

I've even started collecting relics—which is just a fancy word for old items of religious significance—from my personal saints. They are tangible reminders of the power of their faith. I have the personal Bible used by two of my childhood pastors. Though both of these individuals have passed, their legacy remains alive in their impact on my faith. Both of their Bibles are filled with their handwritten notes, and there have been some moments where the simple act of holding their Bibles has been more transformational to my faith than the words those Bibles contain.

One of my most prized "relics" is a nurse's folder that contains my own handwritten scribbles, penned as I sat on the floor outside my father-in-law's triage room on Christmas Eve as a medical team fought to save his life after a massive stroke. I used those notes to preach the candlelight service that he was to lead three hours later. He survived, but those notes are a reminder to me of the powerful feeling of God's presence that night in the midst of trauma.

These people, their stories, and these tangible reminders of them are my spiritual lifeline, buoys in storms of biblical proportions, marking the way back to safe harbor.

Reflect

1. How do you feel about the idea of "saints" after reading this chapter?
2. What living celebrity (musician, artist, academic, athlete, and so on) is a saint in your household? Why?

3. If you know any saints of the church, who is your favorite?
4. If you could select one person from your family to be a recognized saint, living or dead, who would it be and why?
5. Reflect on, and then share, some of your or your family's Ebenezers.
6. If you were named a saint, what would you be the patron of? For what would you be remembered? What food would be eaten at your remembrance feast?

10 Feasts and Fasts

> After a good dinner one can forgive anybody, even one's own relatives.
>
> —Oscar Wilde

The monks at the Abbey of the Genesee make bread; that is what they *do*—though I did see one mowing the lawn during the week, so I guess they do that as well.

But the point of this particular order of monks—the Cistercian Order of the Strict Observance, or "Trappists"—is to be contemplatives. In short, they are *be*-ers rather than *do*-ers. But even monks must make a living, so these monks both *be* and *do*. And their *do*ing is baking bread.

White. Wheat. Rye. Multigrain. Sunflower. Raisin Cinnamon. Gingerbread. Maple Cinnamon. Apple Spice.

It is good bread, *very* good bread.

There are three meals a day in the Bethlehem Retreat House, and each are prepared by the House Mother, who also happens to be the house cook. The dining room—or Refectory, as the monks call it—is the first thing you see as you enter the Retreat House. It is positioned at the end of a long hallway opposite the front door.

The Refectory lights are always on and its doors are always open. There may be a metaphor there somewhere.

Though small, the Refectory still somehow manages to comfortably contain three rows of impossibly long wooden tables. The two outside tables are surrounded on all sides by wooden chairs where those on retreat sit shoulder-to-shoulder in the sharing of a common meal. The center table is the serving station, and today it is bursting at the seams with bowls, baskets, casserole dishes, and of course, an assortment of the monks' homemade bread. I am immediately struck by the realization that I have seen this table before. It is the very same table that my grandmother would often fill with her own dazzling array of food.

I was immediately transported back to the most important table I ever sat at.

Breaking Bread Together

My grandparents had a big family, raising seven children in a very small house. By the time I came along, the family had long outgrown the dining table. Like the table in the Refectory, my grandparents' table was now used more for serving and less for seating.

Grandma never seemed to mind the extreme disparity between the size of the family and the size of the table. I believe that she secretly enjoyed having more serving space anyway. For Grandma, an empty table was a challenge waiting to be conquered … waiting to be filled. In her mind, more space simply meant more room for food.

No one left my grandmother's house hungry.

Sons, daughters, salespeople, and strangers always found a listening ear and a seat at the table, anytime day or night, whether or not it was mealtime. Like clockwork, 15 minutes after arrival, every visitor would find themselves with fork in hand staring at a full plate of food.

Grandma's table always seemed to be filled with food … and people.

As I got older, I began to notice that many people seemed to prefer doing their business in person around the table rather than by phone. I noticed that people would drop in, often unannounced, *because* of the food. I noticed it because I did the same thing! There was no reason too small to make a trip to Grandma's table.

Things were different in my house.

As the family grew, we seemed to spend less and less time around the table together. Our family meals had been all but decimated by ball games, work schedules, and church events. The final nail in the coffin of family mealtime came in the form of a large box my father brought home one summer afternoon. He said that it would save us time and money, and I had not seen him quite so excited in a very long time. With great fanfare he revealed the box's contents, a microwave oven. The first microwaves were quite large, and this one was no different. It was an enormous beast of a device, and it quickly ate our family mealtimes.

In the years after the arrival of the microwave oven, our family seemed to find more excuses to be at Grandma's house around dinnertime. We joined the parade of others who hoped to experience the wonder and beauty of a fully functioning table. My grandmother did eventually get a microwave—bought by some well-meaning but shortsighted person—but we were all lucky that it did not change her life, setting mostly unused except as a coffee warmer. Her table, on the other hand, was never idle.

There was a time when I believed that it was the amazing made-from-scratch food that brought so many wanderers to my grandmother's table, but now I am not so sure. My grandparents had the good fortune of growing up in one of America's poorest counties. There, in the Appalachian foothills of Eastern Kentucky, they learned that some of life's most important moments aren't bought but served across a table with family and friends. As such, their family life was built together around the table, and they invited others to join them. While the food was good, the meal was just an appetizer into the true main course: my grandparents. Family, friend, sales representative, and stranger returned to the table time and again to experience the warm fellowship of these two simple saints.

Each day at the Abbey, I passed by a baptismal font in order to enter the sanctuary. It stands as a silent sentry to worship, reminding all who come that entry to the church is gained only by way of baptism.

Much like the monastery, my grandmother's house taught an important lesson through layout. It is the only house I have ever seen where the front door opens into the kitchen. What some might see as a design flaw seemed to me quite fitting.

Everyone who came in, came by way of the table.

Bread as a Symbol of Hospitality and Community

While eating in silence at the Refectory over the smell of freshly baked monks' bread, I finally understand what my grandmother has long known: a table filled with people and bread is the heart and hope of the home.

In the ancient Near East, bread was the symbol of hospitality. To withhold bread from guests or travelers was not just considered inhospitable, it was downright rude and offensive. One of the most overlooked themes in the biblical text is the ongoing importance of breaking and sharing bread; its sweet smell wafts through the pages of Scripture:

- Abram made bread for the three heavenly guests who traveled to bring news of a baby of hope.
- Bread, in the form of manna, sustained the Hebrews for 40 years of wilderness wandering.
- Ravens brought bread to the prophet Elijah in the darkest moments of his depression and fear.
- Jesus was born in Bethlehem, "The House of Bread."
- Jesus miraculously multiplied bread … twice.
- Jesus often broke bread with outcasts, tax collectors, and other notorious sinners.
- Bread was the key symbol in the Last Supper, and became a critical component in the ongoing remembrance and enactment of his death.

Bread has *always* given humanity the clearest picture of Jesus: his hospitality, his provision, his healing, his divinity, his love, his redemption, and his incarnation. If Jesus had a vocation other than carpenter (or Savior of the world), I think that it would likely be master bread maker. It should come as little surprise that the Early Church saw bread as essential to believers' faith.

In the first days after the ascension of Jesus and the fall of the Holy Spirit, there were more questions than answers about the future of the ragtag group of Christ-followers who called themselves "The Way." The one thing that did not seem to be in question during the early days of the church was how to spend their time.

As discussed earlier, Acts 2 points out that early Christians devoted themselves to only five things: the apostles' teaching, prayer, fellowship, sharing resources, and the "breaking of bread." It is important that we remember that these were not extracurricular activities squeezed into the family's free time on Sunday afternoons or Thursday nights. These five pursuits encompassed the entirety of their worship. They pursued prayer, fellowship, the apostles' teaching, sharing resources, and breaking of bread. As I have pointed out, we must resist the urge to assume that the reference to the breaking of bread is a creative way of saying *communion* because it primarily indicates that they shared a meal.

The earliest worship services took place over a meal. For the Early Church, there was little if any difference between a food-meal and the communion-meal. They were one and the same!

Worship Time Was Mealtime

The best New Testament example of the worship/meal practice is seen when the Apostle Paul pens a letter to the church meeting in the town in Corinth and addresses their less-than–Christ-like mealtime habits. These church meal events were not just an opportunity for potluck fellowship after a worship gathering; the meal *was* their regular worship gathering.

No pulpits.

No pews.

No passing of communion trays filled with shot glasses of grape juice.

The Early Church had meal-meetings, which it referred to as "Agape Feasts" or "Love Feasts."

Love Feasts were not a brief blip in the long span of church history either. Love Feasts continued to be the primary way that Christians worshipped for generations, perhaps several centuries. This helps to explain why Paul was so concerned about meal practices in the Early Church. To leave someone out of the meal (as was happening in Corinth) effectively shut them out of the life of the faith community itself. These mealtime disagreements became the church's first *worship wars*.

Jesus got into a few squabbles over meals himself. The Gospels indicate that he was always under the microscope over how he ate, what he ate, and with whom he ate it. It seems that he was always upsetting someone or another by eating the wrong things, in the wrong way, with the wrong people. To understand why, you need to know that in the 1st century, meals mattered … a lot. Eating was a very intimate act; your dinner company spoke volumes about social status and acceptance.

In Jesus' day, it was only acceptable to sup with those who were of equal social status and belief systems. Kings did not share table fellowship with commoners; religious leaders did not share table fellowship with sinners. This begins to explain the ongoing outrage over whom Jesus had over for dinner, and outraged they were! In one particularly revealing moment, a group of frustrated onlookers turn to Jesus' disciples in exasperation and thinly veiled disgust, saying: "Why does your teacher eat with such scum?!"[1]

Jesus regularly broke with social conventions surrounding mealtime, sharing table fellowship with those that the world considered to be undeserving scum.

His mealtime practices were considered unbecoming of a rabbi, especially one of his status. Jesus' table manners (or lack thereof) were downright offensive to nearly everyone's sensibilities, and his playing fast and loose with the rules enraged more than a few religious people of his day. His actions made their blood boil and became one the key cornerstones of their hatred for him. It has been said that Jesus was killed because of what he ate.

[1] Matthew 9:11.

A little dramatic, perhaps, but mostly true.

The Early Church practice of communal meals for worship—where everyone was equal at the table—was merely a continuation of the shocking precedent set by Jesus himself. At the table of Christians, social status was erased and eating together in unity became a real-world example of the unbelievable uniqueness of The Way of Jesus. Therefore, it should come as no surprise why the Early Church chose to worship around a table. Listen to this firsthand description of a worship meal just after the time of Christ:

> *We do not recline until we have first tasted of prayer to God; as much is eaten as to satisfy the hungry; only as much is drunk as is proper to the chaste. They are satisfied as those who remember that they have to praise God even in the night; they talk as those who know that the Lord is listening. After water for washing the hands, and lights, each is invited to sing publicly to God as able from Holy Scripture or from their own ability; thus how each has drunk is put to the test. Similarly prayer closes the feast.*[2]

If you were paying careful attention, you may have noticed how closely their mealtime worship gatherings mirror the worship services of today.

Mealtime Brought People Together

At the table, these early Christians prayed, sang, and sometimes sat late into the night. It all certainly sounds like a typical church potluck. And while on the surface, nothing about these Love Feasts seems subversive, they were. With each meal, the Christians chipped away at the social stratification of society that separated

[2] Tertullian, *Apology*, 39.17–18.

different social classes, ethnicities, and other barriers culture put in place between people.

At the table, all were one.

At the table, they were a group of people who did not otherwise belong together, sharing life together. Not only were they sharing radical table fellowship, but they were pouring out libations in honor and remembrance of a Jesus—a crucified victim of the Emperor's rule—rather than to the Emperor.

It was all *very* countercultural, even subversive.

But as you learned earlier, the Early Church didn't just center the table and food for worship, they centered meals elsewhere. One of the most notable was funerary meals at the tombs of the martyrs, each year, on the date of their birth into Jesus' presence. These annual celebrations of remembrance offered the opportunity to participate in a family meal, share stories, worship together, and look forward to the great Wedding Banquet of the Lamb where the Christian community expected to be reunited with Jesus and the growing list of martyrs.

Meals with the martyrs became so popular that they were added to local church calendars as "Feast Days," which were special days set aside to eat and remember, much like they did with Jesus on Sundays, eat and remember at the Table. The Feast Days to the Martyr Saints took their position alongside the more universal feasts celebrating Advent, Easter, Epiphany, and Pentecost.

It might be said that the Early Church formed a culture of feasting.

The Role of Fasting

The table was central to the Early Church, but so was knowing when to avoid it. The revelry and celebration that came as part of the communal meals and feast days were balanced by regular days and seasons of fasting. Though it is difficult to imagine, fasting was just as popular a practice as feasting. The Early Church had a passion for fasting.

The most famous season of fasting in the Early Church is still practiced by many today: Lent. This ancient journey of self-deprivation was an opportunity for the entire community of Christ-followers to come together and join new converts in their ritual fast before baptism on Easter. And lest we believe that early Christians only fasted from chocolate or carbonation for 40 days a year, they also commonly fasted twice a week, year-round, every Wednesday and Friday, as a reminder of Jesus' own sacrifice.

Though the church's commitment to fasting has continued throughout the centuries and remains a key spiritual practice—albeit in a greatly diminished way as compared to its ancient past—the primary place of feasting was relatively short-lived.

The church kept the fasting but lost the feasting.

Let that sit for a moment.

We replaced tables with pews and pass-arounds with pulpits. We moved the meal to a few minutes of sipped fruit from the vine and tasteless bread. We abandoned the meal as the centerpiece of communal worship, relegating the "breaking of bread" to a short, programmed segment within a larger service filled with other items often deemed far more important. And while many churches still put "Feast Days" on their official calendar, the actual feasting all but fell away from these days.

The church pushed back from the table.

Though the Abbey and its worship space are only a short walk away, the Retreat House at which I am staying has its own chapel as well. It is the second door on the right just after you enter the living quarters. Though it is small, the chapel is larger than you might expect for a house. It looks like the sanctuary of a small country church, and it is decorated about the same, which is to say, not well.

Rows of pews stretch from the rear of the chapel to the front altar, and they are beautiful, their wood a lightly stained oak and their padding—like the carpet—a deep shade of crimson. Neither the pews nor the carpet seem very worn, meaning the chapel sees little use. There is a large crucifix on the wall behind the altar, and it is awkwardly large, overpowering the space in which it resides. There are several icons of the Virgin Mary scattered around the room as well.

During my initial tour, the House Mother proudly noted that this chapel is open for use by people of all faith communities. I nearly laugh aloud—which would be very against the rules of this silent retreat—as I try to imagine this very Catholic chapel being used by other faiths. I tried to imagine Protestants, Muslims, and Hare Krishnas attempting to use this space for anything other than Catholic mass. I couldn't imagine it at all. As such, I assumed that the chapel sat empty all of the time. Non-Catholics weren't likely to use it, and Catholics had a glorious Abbey up the road that they could use instead.

Imagine my surprise on noticing a lady in the chapel very early on my second morning in the house.

I guess I was wrong, I thought.

There she sat, in the third pew next to the aisle, proving me wrong.

Maybe I should give this little chapel a chance.

But I couldn't give the chapel a chance because each time I checked in, there she was, and I am relatively certain that she had not moved an inch since I had first seen her.

What perseverance! I thought. *What was her story?*

She was holding a Bible—the old, thick type with crinkly pages and black thumb indexes to show each individual book. It was worn, very worn, and she was holding it up in front of her face. She looked to be talking to it, or perhaps reading from it and praying. Whatever she was doing, she was doing with fervor.

She failed to join the house members for lunch, making it two meals now missed. I was baffled and intrigued. Perhaps she was fasting.

With each passing service of prayer at the Abbey that day, my mind wandered to the little chapel at the Retreat House.

Was she still there? Did she ever move?

Every time I looked in on her, the answer was always: *yes, and apparently no.*

With each passing hour she seemed to become increasingly animated and—to my eye—distraught. At some point during the waning hours of the day, she had dropped her Bible and began rocking back and forth as if in prayer. Her Bible lay disheveled beside her, as though it was no longer of any help to what she was enduring.

There she remained, into the night, past the time that I retired to bed.

At the Abbey, each day begins with 2:00 a.m. Vigils for those who wish to join the monks in the day's first hour of prayer. As I arose, dressed, and headed into the night to make my way to the Abbey, the thick fog of the morning mirrored my own cloudy mind. I had forgotten the plight of the lady, until I was startled again by her presence as I passed the chapel at 3:00 a.m.

There she was.

Same spot.

Still rocking.

Has she moved at all?

Has she eaten?

Questions began to fill my groggy brain. Her perseverance not only amazed me, it also scared me.

Was she okay?

I wasn't entirely sure that she *was* okay. I could see that she was now clinging to a rosary, praying one by one through the beads, rocking as she progressed, then beginning again. She now seemed to me to be very tormented. Her face seemed to be filled with pain and agony. I contemplated entering the chapel to help or going to find help, but who would I wake at this hour … and for what reason?

She may be hurt, but she is hurting no one.

I wonder what darkness fills her soul.

It must be very deep.

My mind quickly raced through the various possibilities.

Had she lost someone dear?

Maybe there was some deep pain or trauma?

Was it a divorce that broke her soul?

An abortion or rape?

Homicide?

I was fairly certain of the presence of tears.

She sat there through the night, nervously thumbing the beaded cross in her hands and praying. I checked in on her regularly, captured by her perseverance and pain.

By the second day, I had come to think of that third pew as "her place." I would have been surprised—if not more than a little disappointed—to have not found her in it.

I *was* becoming tremendously worried about her though.

Had anyone checked in on her?

Had anyone else even noticed her?

Did she have a roommate at the Retreat House?

I thought about taking her food, but decided against it. It seemed to me that it was the job of the House Mother to assist those who were either too deep in prayer to eat or who were homicidal murderers on the lam, whichever she may be.

I began to find any excuse necessary to pass by the chapel; no reason was too small to look in the window for an update. I was, admittedly, more than a little obsessed.

Little changed that day, until dinner. On my way to the Refectory for the evening meal I looked into the chapel—as I had done countless times over the past two days—and to my surprise, just as spontaneously as she had arrived, she was gone. I stretched to see if she had fallen, or worse, had died. She was nowhere in the chapel. Over the past day I had begun to wonder if she was a spirit.

Puzzled, I made my way to the Refectory.

Those who had gathered for the evening meal were already in silent prayer. Joining them, I found it difficult to focus on prayer as my mind wandered to the lady and her plight. I took the chair closest to the Refectory door, which was positioned in such a way as to have a perfect view out the door and down the main hall of the Retreat House—a hall whose carpet was a bit more threadbare from my pacing to and from the chapel window over the last several days.

I liked this dining seat in particular because it had a perfect view of the front door at the end of the hall. The front door featured a unique window arrangement in the shape of a cross. At dinnertime, light spilled through the cross, illuminating the hallway with the wonderful golden hues of sunset. If, like today, no one sat across from me, then I could spend the meal looking at the cross, thinking and praying.

I often found myself losing a half hour at the meal, just sitting and staring into the light of the cross, contemplating Christ and *his* cross.

What the ...?!

Imagine my surprise when—lost in deep contemplation of Christ and his suffering—Jesus himself stepped out of the chapel door and in front of the cross! My eyes tried to refocus and process the moment, unable to keep up with my head.

God!?

My heart stalled.

I nearly shouted—which would have been decidedly against house rules. Lest you think my cry would have been one of great joy, I must tell you that sheer terror was all that I felt in that moment. In the blinding light of the cross, I was unable to tell if this was an apparition or something else.

The figure, blurred by the blinding light of the cross, began to make its way down the hall toward me.

OMG, OMG, OMG!

Were it not for the shock of the moment having seized every muscle in my body, I would have jumped from the seat, overturned the table, and run.

I am glad that I did not though because it wasn't Jesus … it was her.

It was *the* woman.

Except, it wasn't a *her* at all.

She was a man.

The woman who had kept vigil for so very long had been a man.

It took a while for that fact to register.

She was a he, and the *he* looked very much like Jesus to me.

He was tall, very tall, with a beard and beautiful hair that flowed down his back.

I sat motionless as he fixed a small plate of rice and a piece of bread and then proceeded to take a seat ***across the table from me***!

I just stared at him.

I couldn't eat; I could barely breathe.

Jesus—which I have taken to calling him—looked up a few times, smiled, and then went back to his plate.

Then without a word, he got up and left.

I never saw him again.

Reconstructing Meals

I never saw him again, but I have reflected on that meal a great deal in the meantime. I wish that I would have had the presence of mind to reach out to him and ask him questions. There were some things that I desperately wanted to know.

First and foremost, was he *really* Jesus?

I cannot say for certain, but I can say that in the years since the Abbey, I have begun to see Jesus rather regularly in the faces of those with whom I share a meal.

After the Abbey, my family began to make mealtimes more important. For one meal a day, we turned off the television, turned over the phones, and began to get to know one another. Soon, we realized that the meal was strengthening our family bonds, and our children were becoming more secure in themselves and in their faith because of the conversations that took place at the table. They began to see how their own stories were weaved into the fabric of our larger family story and the greater story of God.

The table quickly became the most central and sacred piece of furniture in our home, and when COVID took us from our regular church gatherings, the table became our central place of eating *and* worship.

Like the Early Church, mealtime was worship time.

We fielded deep conversations at the table that felt out of place in other places, and at the table we found safety in asking our toughest questions, be they theological, relational, or something else. It wasn't long before our children began to protect this mealtime in a more fiercely loyal way than even I had done. Our table provided the natural and necessary location for spiritual conversations, prayer needs, and spiritual practices to be shared and lived out. Even in the late teen years, they still enforce our family mealtime and remind my wife and me if we lapse.

And the table didn't just provide that for my family, it began to provide it for me personally. When the institutional church had rejected my questions and made me feel like an outsider, I knew that I was always welcome at the family table.

Being welcomed unconditionally at the family table finally helped me see that I had *always* been unconditionally welcomed at Jesus' table as well. The same Jesus who saved a seat for Judas and served him the Bread and Cup had done the same for me, inviting me to sup.

No.

Questions.

Asked.

Just come as you are, Kevin … and eat.

The table fed me and eventually healed my faith. One bowl of chicken and dumplings at a time, I returned to God. Heart full; stomach fuller.

We longed for other people to experience this kind of table fellowship, so we began looking for people to invite to join us at our table. Since the story of the Bible, Jesus, and the Abbey revolve around bread, we purchased the best bread maker that we could afford. That way, there would always be fresh homemade bread at the table for guests or to give away to others. When we give away these loaves, we often share how important bread is to the story of God and to the story of our family. We tell them how Jesus was born in Bethlehem, a place called "The House of Bread," and how my faith was reconstructed in the fields and fellowship of an Abbey that baked bread.

The centrality and sacredness of the table has been the philosophy that our family has guarded and nurtured in the years since the Abbey. No one is barred from our table, and we will intentionally invite those with whom we might have difficulty or disagreement over (or out) to a meal. I have often invited those on the margins of faith, the outcasts of Christianity, the rejects to our table. They are almost always surprised, having never been invited into the home of a Christian.

Along the way, I realized that the table was the best place for healing the most broken things in my life.

Dinnertime became so central to our family story and our faith that, a few years ago, I bought a truckload of cedar and hand-built a family table and matching benches with my boys. It is the most important piece of furniture that we own, and the memories made around the table are as irreplaceable as the table itself. When building it, we made sure it was long enough to allow for guests to join anytime, without notice, just as Grandma would have liked.

Reflect

1. What is your favorite kind of bread? Why?
2. Tell the story of one of your favorite meals.
3. Tell the story of a very difficult meal.
4. What is the most difficult part of family, friend, or business meals for you?
5. How were the meal habits in your house different during childhood from your meals today? How are they similar?

6. Chapter 9 discussed the idea of "family saints." Spend some time creating an imaginary meal of remembrance in honor of one person's life. Use the following prompts:

(a) What foods would be served?
(b) What stories would be told?
(c) What songs would be played?
(d) What smells would be present?
(e) What objects would be displayed?
(f) Who would be invited?

11 Catechism

Words don't go away, they just echo around.

—Jane Goodall

"Catechesis happens."

I looked up from my journal to see a not-so-silent monk having a not-so-quiet conversation with a lady in the lobby of the Abbey.

"Catechesis happens," he shout-whispered just a bit louder than before.

I wondered if the aging monk had any idea of the root of that phrase. Judging by the slight grin on his face, I believe that he did. The woman most assuredly did not, though, scribbling down the phrase on a piece of paper as though she were receiving a new revelation of the inerrant word of God in that very moment.

I did my best to stifle a laugh, but I must have made a sound of some sort because the monk looked around as if to see if anyone had overheard what he had said. I tried to look away, but he made direct eye contact with me, giving a half wink with another grin.

This monk was clearly passionate about catechesis. I'm not sure if his wink was because he thought that I knew a lot about catechesis or because he was somehow aware that I didn't.

At its simplest, *catechesis* is the process of instructing someone in the basics of the faith. It is the embedding of a religion's core tenets into a believer.

While I would not say that the monks and I had become best friends over the week, I had begun to recognize a few of them by name and even think of them as a sort of extended family.

When I wasn't in the Sanctuary or the Refectory, I spent my time sitting in the Abbey's common area, journaling. My heart was so filled with emotions that pen-to-paper felt like the best way to process all of my struggles with the church and my place in it.

So I sat and bled on page after page of paper, transferring my grief and mourning at the state of the church and the trauma it brought to me in an act of emotional catharsis.

Each day, I sat in the same seat, at the end of the same couch, looking out the same window. As the days went by, I wore through several pencils and several decades of mounting spiritual distress. I sat there so long that my backside left what looked to be a permanent indention in the leather couch.

I looked down at my journal and back up at the monk.

He just continued to stare at me.

Oh … he wants me to write that down.

I laughed, but did it:

Catechesis happens.

Human beings are always being formed by someone or something. The question is not so much "*Are* we being formed," but rather "*By what* are we being formed?"

As the week wore on, sitting there in my butt-print, I realized that over the course of my short time at the Abbey, the couch had started to become formed to me, and I had begun to be formed by the rhythms of the ancient church's faith formation practices. The person who had entered the Abbey at the beginning of the week was not the person who would be leaving. The question wasn't "Had I been formed?" but rather "To what extent?"

… and was it enough to rescue my faith?

Catechism in the Early Church

Just to make sure that we are on the same page, a *catechism* is a statement of belief, and *catechesis* is the process of teaching it.

I initially hesitated to mention the word *catechism*—let alone devote a chapter to it—as many recovering religious fundamentalists like me have a love/hate relationship with the concept of catechism (without all of the love). The word brings up images of endless rows of Catholic parochial students, reciting by rote, the call-and-response answers to the (in)famous Baltimore Catechism.

And while the words *Catholic* and *catechism* seem to go hand in hand, many Protestant religious movements have written and taught their own central statements of religious belief as well.

For example, you may have heard of the venerable Heidelberg Catechism, Luther's Small Catechism, or the Westminster

Larger/Shorter Catechism. Even more conservative Christian sects—which usually eschew more traditional models of formation—often supply catechism curriculum to their private and homeschool venues.

The word *catechism* comes from the word *catechesis* out of the Greek verb *katēcheō*, a general word used in the New Testament for teaching or instruction of others. But it also carries with it the idea "to echo."

The Early Church chose this term to communicate its hope for how to best hand off the teachings of Jesus from one person to another. Much like a baton passed in a race, catechesis is the process of handing off the teachings from one person to the next.

Early catechism teachers became known as *catechists*, or literally "echoes/echoers." This developed into a very intentional form of Christian formation where a teacher would work to ensure that essential teachings of the Christian faith were echoed in the life of a new converts. Though the Early Church never defined a definitive procedure for catechizing converts, four distinct stages eventually developed.

Those who were interested in becoming a follower of The Way of Jesus were called *Inquirers*. They were welcomed as an observer of the ways of Jesus and were often assigned a sponsor who was responsible to guide the prospective convert through the process—if they chose to pursue following Jesus—and testify on their behalf. If approved, the Inquirer would join the catechumenate.

In the second phase, the converts—now called the *Catechumen*—entered a structured time of intentional instruction that lasted from one to three years. Yes, up to three full years of instruction before being considered full converts! And though many regarded catechumens to be Christians, they were yet to be fully received as part of the faith community. For instance, Catechumens could not participate in the sacraments of baptism or the Eucharist.

As shown in the illustration, this period of instruction generally focused on:

- Scripture and the Trinity as the foundation of the Christian life.
- The Creed (Rule of Faith), The Lord's Prayer (Rule of Prayer), and the 10 Commandments (Rule of Life).
- The Spiritual Life and the church.
- Christian maturity.

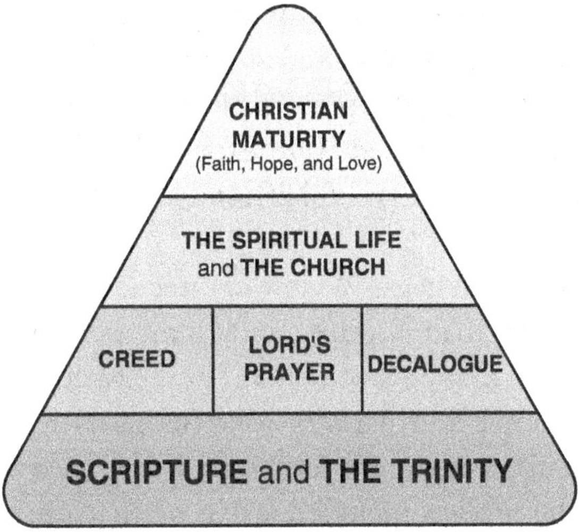

Upon satisfactory completion of instruction, Catechumens were admitted to the final step before baptism.

The third step, the *Candidate* phase, is where things begin to get exciting. This phase traditionally commenced with the beginning of Lent in preparation for baptism at the Easter Vigil. The 40 days before Easter offered the Candidates an opportunity to center themselves spiritually before being fully accepted into the church. Lent came to *be* Lent as a result of many in the church community deciding to join new Candidates in this season of deep reflection and repentance, all of which culminated with their baptism during the Easter Vigil, most usually at sunrise on Easter Sunday morning, gender-segregated and naked, three times professing belief in Father, Son, and Spirit before each of three immersions.

Immediately upon baptism the newly *Initiated* were anointed, prayed over by laying on of hands, celebrated, and officially inducted into the community through the partaking in the Eucharist. Until this point, converts had neither experienced the Eucharist nor had they been catechized regarding it. The mysteries of the meal—combined with full and final admission to the community—all intersected at Easter.

In a sense, though, the process of catechization had only just begun. The newly initiated were expected to continue to conform to Christ, model a faithful life, and lead others to knowledge of Christ.

Unlike our often negative view of catechesis, the Early Church saw it as far more than just the mindless memorization of church doctrines and statements of belief. They saw education as relational, communal, and participatory. Sponsors led the process, the entire faith community joined in at key moments (such as Lent), and the process included active participation in key rites of passage along the way.

Catechesis was taken so seriously that it is highly likely that the intentional and ongoing use of catechesis was the foremost reason that the early Christian movement did not die. In fact, it thrived.

But as effective as catechesis was for forming faith, the church slowly lost sight of its power as a tool for transformation. By the

1500s, the intentional catechizing of children and adults had become a rare occurrence, and a church that had at one time been passionate about developing handles for faith through doctrine began to focus on other priorities. Spiritual formation, if it happened at all, increasingly took place during sermons, liturgy, hymnography, processions, and art. These do teach, of course, but it wasn't enough.

Those who desired deep formation—which historically had been offered through catechetical programs—were now forced to enter the monastic life (like the monks who milled around me every day at the Abbey) or go without. The largely uncatechized church of the Middle Ages became the fertile soil for serious errors in terms of doctrine, faith, and practice, making the period very dark indeed and ready for reformation.

One of the primary tools that fueled the success of the Reformation was Luther's *Small Catechism,* Calvin's *Geneva Catechism,* the *Heidelberg Catechism,* and a new counter-catechism from the Roman Catholic Church. The newfound focus on historic catechesis, alongside the power of the printing press to distribute catechisms, ended up stoking the fires of the Reformation itself.

Though the Reformation fires were stoked by an emphasis on embedding the faith in followers of Christ and then echoing that faith into future generations, 500 years later the church finds itself with a population that is largely uncatechized in even the most basic beliefs of Christianity.

This had become part of my frustration as a pastor.

There was no way that I could undo centuries of bad theology in my church when the broader church culture was reinforcing the errors every day on social media, in books, through conferences, and through political conversations.

Catechesis happens.

Catechized by Love

The church was being catechized by its preferred cable news channel and political party, thinking it was Christianity. The loudest influencers on social media had more input to their thinking than Matthew, Mark, Luke, or John combined. But worse than what was coming from outside of the church, the strongest and most respected voices from within Christendom were often wrong. The greatest threat to faith formation wasn't culture—which is so often the target of evangelical rhetoric—but the church itself, and more specifically, the church's unwillingness to clearly teach and instruct its people in the basics of Christianity.

The church being its own worst enemy isn't a new problem. The first trouble the church ever encountered was from the inside, when a couple with the rather unfortunate names of Ananias and Sapphira tried to short-circuit the love and generosity of the church.[1]

A review of 2,000 years of church history will reveal that most of the pickles that the church has gotten itself into over the years are because its people—in one way or another—tried to short-circuit the love and generosity of Jesus, which is supposed to flow freely through the church.

I looked up from my notebook where I had scrawled the words "Catechesis happens" in the margins of the page I was writing. The rest of the page was filled with painful reflections on the church I was then pastoring. I had been preaching love, but LGBTQ+ members had sat in my office and cried over feeling unsafe in our groups. I had spent years building racial bridges in the community, but several of my elders were intent on tearing them down. I had pleaded for the opportunity to be able to lead the church against the increasingly treacherous tide

[1]Acts 5:1–11.

of Evangelicalism, but I was regularly rebuffed because "that is where the people and money are."

But how could I blame others? I realized that part of the problem was me. Perhaps, were I being honest, the *largest* part of the problem was me.

I had done a great job catechizing them in the distinctive doctrines of our denomination and how we differed from the church down the street. I had spent a great deal of my time discipling them in the finer points of our official Statement of Belief. Our Membership Classes were filled with all of the things that they needed to avoid if they were to maintain membership.

But had I ever taught them to love?

Had I ever catechized them in generosity?

I had taught them Paul, but had I ever shown them Jesus?

Our enormous parking lot sat in the shadow of a three-story sports and education building that had been built before my arrival. When the building was erected, the church decided to place this verse on the side for all who visited the church to see as their welcome:

You are my friends, if you do what I command. (John 15:14)

Aside from being the most seeker-insensitive verse that I've ever seen as a first impression from a church, I don't think that the congregation ever really understood Jesus' point. But I couldn't blame them, so many Christians don't.

Far too many Christ-followers believe that God has commanded them to fight against women's health and LGBTQ+ rights. Many Christians are convinced that they are called by God to vote for a certain political party and weigh in on every political argument on behalf of the Almighty. They are convinced their job is to vote God's person into political office or sway the Supreme Court. Many who are committed to Jesus see their sole Kingdom mission as being soldiers in a war on sexuality and gender issues.

But I never recalled Jesus saying any of this.

I simply recalled the time when an expert approached Jesus and asked him what the most important commandment was. And there were a *lot* of commands. More than 600 laws, sublaws, and attached rabbinical explanations. If Jesus answers, then he's busted because they treated them all equally.

"Teacher, which is the most important commandment in the law of Moses?" he asked.

"Jesus replied, 'You must love the Lord your God with all your heart, all your soul, and all your mind.' This is the first and greatest commandment. A second is equally important: 'Love your neighbor as yourself.' The entire law and all the demands of the prophets are based on these two commandments."[2]

So Jesus says, "all of them are important … but really they all can be lived out and fulfilled in just doing these two: Love God. Love Others."

Brilliant. That was easy.

And just in case they missed it, Jesus doubles down on this with his disciples at the Last Supper, telling them: "So now I am giving you a new commandment: Love each other. Just as I have loved you, you should love each other. Your love for one another will prove to the world that you are my disciples."[3]

So here we have it again. Jesus said all of the commands could be wrapped up in: Love God. Love others.

And now Jesus reiterates that by saying that this love they show to each other will prove they are his followers.

Notice, it isn't a person's adherence or allegiance to the Bible, or a political party, or even a specific doctrine that determines whether a person is a true follower.

It's love.

[2] Matthew 22:36–40.

[3] John 13:34–35.

I looked down at my notebook one more time.

"Catechesis happens."

And it hit me.

We are being catechized by the wrong things. Doctrines and beliefs are important to a point, but Jesus made it clear that his people would be identified by how they loved.

Tears began to stream down my face as I realized how deeply I longed for a church that had been catechized by love rather than law and legalism. I longed to be surrounded by people who had embedded grace not guilt, mercy not meanness, into their statements of belief. I wanted to be a part of a community that said, "Love Your Neighbor" and didn't tack on "... by telling them truth."

Jesus didn't add a thing; why would we ever dare?!

Jesus never qualified his statements about love, and I was exhausted of a Christianity that did.

I looked up at the monk, caught his eye, and smiled.

He dipped his head just a bit, as if taking a bow.

Somehow he had known what I needed to hear.

Reconstructing Catechism

In the years since the Abbey, I found myself regularly going through the exercise of writing my personal statement of belief (catechism). While items came and went from the list with each revision, I began to notice a trend. I was using less and less paper each time.

Over the years, I have removed more things from my statement of belief than I have added, and with each passing year, I whittle it down more and more, yet somehow the strength of my belief grows. And I don't believe less; I believe more today than I have ever believed in the hope of Jesus.

It's not as though I have no firmly held doctrinal beliefs by which to catechize. I do, and I discuss some of them in the next chapter. But, like Jesus, I have realized that less is more. This taught me an important lesson.

The most important thing in the Jesus Catechism is love. Everything else, no matter how important, is secondary.

Love God. Love Others. Nothing more. Nothing less.

This is the catechism that I want to pass on to my children.

Talks around the family table often circle around beliefs. The kids bring questions about science and sexuality, technology and theology, relationships and wrongdoing to family dinners. Rather than answer the questions with firm statements from our church's statement of belief, we often work to figure out our own family's Statement of Belief on the topic. We use our experience, reliance on the Spirit, and often a nearby Bible to flesh out our own belief as a family.

And if everyone doesn't agree in the end, that is okay! There are tens of thousands of Christian denominations. So if we end up with two different opinions at the table, we don't stress about it too much.

More than anything, we want to be known as a family that draws the boundaries of the Kingdom of God wider, not smaller.

Reflect

1. What would others say most forms the kind of person who you are (such as a sports team, a hobby, a specific person, and so on)?
2. How would you describe this phase of your spiritual journey?
3. What do you think is most missing (or underemphasized) from the church's teachings today?
4. Create a personal catechism with at least five statements that describe you.

12 Creeds

> Don't stop believin', hold on to that feelin'.
>
> —Journey

As my time at the Abbey began to draw to its end, I knew that it had changed me, but I was yet unable to fathom the depths of that change or where it might lead me on the road ahead.

I had spent the week being baptized into a very ancient way of faith that was so old that it made my stream of Christianity seem as though it were still in its awkward adolescence. And while I had been taught to fear much of these old ways of forming faith—liturgy, saints, catechism, and the like—I couldn't help but shake the feeling that those lines of thinking were lies that were left over from the infighting of the Great Reformation.

I wondered if the tearing down of all of the old tried-and-true ways of forming Christians—ways that went back to the Apostles themselves—was really reformation or just an angry dismantling of the things that we didn't like.

Was the Reformer's deification of a Paper Pope, the Bible, really all that better than the flesh and blood one?

This wasn't an easy question to answer. Even more complicated, facing my own idolatry of the Bible.

When I became uncomfortably aware that the Bible had not always existed, I refused to believe it. I preferred to imagine that the Holy Book had dropped through a hole in Heaven, straight to us, by way of the pen of the Apostles and the Fab Four authors of the Gospels.

I didn't want to see that it took more than 100 years after Christ for there to be the beginning stages of lists of texts that *could* be divinely inspired. Over 100 years! It was even harder to admit the books included in the Bible would not be agreed on until 200–300 years after Christ, that the process of selecting them was messy, and that the final list has never really been very final. Different branches of Christianity see different books as inspired, and of course, we all believe that ours is the correct list and the others, for whatever reason, are not.

And if you can get past all of that, remember that Gutenberg would not invent the printing press until 1436, meaning that once we had the Bible—whichever version we had—it had to be hand-copied, line by line, page by page, in a painstaking process that extended over 15 months per Bible. Those hand-lettered copies of the Bible were then slowly disseminated to monasteries, cathedrals, and eventually, to local parishes, a process that took centuries.

Before the printing press, if a nonclergy commoner even had local access to a Bible, it is highly unlikely that they would have been allowed to handle it. Most Bibles were kept under lock and key, hidden away or chained to the church lectern. And even if the average person had happened to lay eyes on a Bible during their lifetime, they probably would not have been able to read it. Literacy rates for the first 1,000 years of the Bible's existence were somewhere around 1 in 5 in towns, and far worse (1 in 20) in the countryside.

Was the Bible important? Yes, I still believed that without equivocation.

But it was a wake-up call for me, as a pastor, who had often said, "The Bible is sufficient," to realize that for the first 300 years or so of Christianity, the Bible didn't exist. And for the next 1,000 years or so, relatively few people had access to it.

What was sufficient for them?

This became an even more interesting question when I realized that the greatest growth of Christianity happened in its first few centuries, when there was no Bible at all. How did Christianity grow explosively without a Bible, something seen as so necessary today? How did the Early Church know what was orthodox and unorthodox without a Bible to weigh in? How did the church decide what was within the boundaries of orthodoxy and what was not?

In these contexts, the power of a creed cannot be overstated.

Creeds Confirm Beliefs

"No creed but Christ."

This should have been the motto of my anti-everything childhood church; it was said so much from behind the pulpit. There was such a strong aversion to creeds that any "creedal church" was considered to be anti-Christ and in violation of the Bible. It wasn't until I finally began reading a few of the Early Church creeds for myself that I wondered if any of them had actually read a creed.

For the life of me, I couldn't understand the problem.

A *creed* is simply a summary statement of belief, usually containing the most important core tenets of teaching in the faith. The word *creed* itself comes from the Latin word for "I believe."

While various creeds seek to accomplish different (and sometimes competing) goals, they all are positional statements that put a stake in the ground and proclaim, "THIS is what we believe most!"

In the years before the Bible, the creeds were unimaginably important in ensuring that everyone was on the same page in their basic foundational beliefs about Jesus and God. In fact, creeds were so important to the early years of the church that we have remnants of several in the New Testament.

Here are a few:

Jesus is Lord.
(Romans 10:9)

For there is one body and one Spirit, just as you have been called to one glorious hope for the future. There is one Lord, one faith, one baptism, one God and Father of all, who is over all, in all, and living through all.
(Ephesians 4:4–6)

I passed on to you what was most important and what had also been passed on to me. Christ died for our sins, just as the Scriptures said. He was buried, and he was raised from the dead on the third day, just as the Scriptures said. He was seen by Peter and then by the Twelve. After that, he was seen by more than 500 of his followers at one time, most of whom are still alive, though some have died. Then he was seen by James and later by all the apostles.
(1 Corinthians 15:3–7)

Paul's language in these passages is creedal in nature, and 1 Corinthians even includes an introduction that indicates the declaration was already in circulation as a primary statement of belief in the Early Church. If we take the earliest datings of Paul's letters to be accurate, then it means that the church had already developed creedal statements within five years of Jesus' resurrection.

Whether or not one accepts Paul's words as our earliest creeds, it is clear from history that the Early Church felt the need for creeds and continued to develop and refine them as time went on. Even the eventual development of a canon of Scripture—the Bible—did little to diminish the desire for creedal statements of belief.

Some of the most important early creeds of the church include:

- The Old Roman Symbol (2nd century)
- The Apostles' Creed (2nd–3rd centuries)
- Creed of Nicaea (325 CE)
- The Nicene Creed (325 CE)
- The Chalcedonian Creed (451 CE)
- The Athanasian Creed (500 CE)

Creeds Are Complicated

Creeds are a way to effectively pull together all of the church's teachings into a single, memorable, and cohesive statement. They conveniently cut through an overwhelming amount of doctrine and opinion in order to define what really matters.

In the beginning, creeds were unifying forces. Adherents to the faith were asked to adhere to the creeds because unity in faith and practice was critical at a time when so much was in question. The passing of the Apostles and their authority had brought instability. A rise in intense persecution had brought fear. And an influx of broad diversity (especially in a wave of new converts from non-Jewish pagan backgrounds) threatened to dilute the doctrinal and practical uniqueness of The Way.

The fledgling faith was at risk, but the creeds brought unity.

This may have been part of the reason that my childhood church disliked the creeds. Rather than find our commonalities and places of agreement, many Evangelicals now seek to set the boundaries of faith so small as to condemn everyone but those in their particular pew … and sometimes they aren't so certain of the people in their own pew.

This isn't a new problem. Creeds are not just unifying by nature; they are also divisive. Creeds exclude.

As new understandings of the Christian faith—and especially new perceived heresies—began to form, the church would unite to try to discern the right path and then codify the new dogma into an updated creed. This is why creeds tended to become lengthier over time.

The Old Roman Symbol, one of the earliest creeds, is one of the shortest:

I believe in God the Father almighty;
and in Christ Jesus His only Son, our Lord,
Who was born of the Holy Spirit and the Virgin Mary,
Who under Pontius Pilate was crucified and buried,
on the third day rose again from the dead,
ascended to heaven,
sits at the right hand of the Father,
whence He will come to judge the living and the dead;
and in the Holy Spirit,
the holy Church,
the remission of sins,
the resurrection of the flesh.

In comparison, the later Nicene Creed is three times longer.

The danger in all of this should be quite obvious. There may be a risk in drawing the boundaries of orthodoxy too broad, but there is greater danger in drawing the boundaries too small.

The New Testament gives story after painful story of those who were excluded from the worshipping community but admitted by Jesus into the Kingdom. Religious people have a tendency to exclude people who Jesus did not.

This points to the problem that I was facing with much of my Christianity before arriving at the Abbey. It was more concerned with keeping people out than it was throwing the doors open wide to bring people into the love of God and the safety of the church. Everyone seemed to see themselves as gatekeeper to the Gates of Heaven, but no one could ever seem to agree on the minutia surrounding what kept someone out.

Acceptance over Judgment

As I began to explore theologies and thinking outside of my strict theological sect within Christianity, I began to hear certain phrases repeated from those who feared drawing the boundaries of orthodoxy too broad:

"You just want to let everyone into the Kingdom of God."

Yes, and what is the problem if everyone comes to faith in Jesus?

"You don't care about sin."

No, I do. But I have my hands full just paying attention to my own. Don't you?

"You affirm sin."

No, I just don't affirm your list of sins as being Jesus' or God's list of sins. Let's talk about the differences.

"You don't teach repentance."

No, I do believe that we could do with repentance, if we define it the way the Bible does as a "change of mind." For instance, I'm hoping you will change yours to become more like Christ, just as I attempt to do daily through my own repentance.

"You don't believe in historic Christian beliefs."

Whoa. Hold up. Let's pull out some creeds. How far back do you want to go?!

As the churches I pastored and followed kept adding pages, declarations, and additional doctrines to their statements of belief, I was rewinding time and falling increasingly in love with older and older expressions of faith.

While Evangelicalism was losing its mind over the definition of marriage, human sexuality, the doctrine of "Love Your Neighbor," and the defense of inerrancy, I was finding hope and healing in The Apostles' Creed and the Old Roman Symbol.

In them, I found a Jesus who I could surrender myself to.

I had entered the Abbey discouraged, confused, and unbelievably frustrated. All of the handles that I had held in my faith were in question. It was clear that I had spent decades holding onto the wrong things.

The Abbey had begun to change me, refining my pain into something different, something holy. It felt like my mistakes and missteps were being redeemed and repaired.

I felt peace.

But on the other aside of the Abbey, I instinctively knew that a new storm awaited. Getting here had required letting go of the faulty beliefs and creeds that had become a noose around my neck.

I could no longer believe all of the things that I had been taught to believe. I could no longer teach many of things that I had been teaching. I had to admit that I had been taught wrong, but worse, I was going to have to admit that I taught wrong things to others. I hadn't purposely done it, but now that I could see the errors in my core beliefs, I couldn't unsee it.

I had shouted "No creed but Christ," but I had soaked up many toxic doctrines from the Evangelical stream in which I swam. Many of my beliefs cause very real harm to others, especially in already marginalized and oppressed communities.

Finding peace at the Abbey had required me to let go of my primary creed: The centrality of myself.

But as I faced the journey home as a new and changed person, I realized that I needed a new creed. New beliefs needed to be embedded in my heart and hands. Jesus and his centrality in my life was, of course, still the goal. But I no longer recognized the Jesus I once followed. He was not the Christ of the Bible but one of my own making.

I was tired of teaching "Love Your Neighbor," but then supporting people, politicians, businesses, causes—even churches and Christians—who brought harm to my neighbors.

I needed a new creed.

I needed new words to describe these new feelings I was having, new feelings based in a very, very old faith.

I knew that the journey from the Abbey would lead me to a new creed. And I dared believe that I would find it in Christ, perhaps for the first time in my life.

Reconstructing Creeds

In the years since the Abbey, I have moved from being a non-creedal Christian to being firmly creedal in my thinking. I found that the journey of deconstruction and reconstruction required an anchor. When I felt like a heretic—or was called one by an anonymous troll on social media—it helped to be able to hold onto something broadly accepted by the historic church.

The later creeds felt too time-based to the doctrinal dilemmas of the day, so I kept moving increasingly closer to the Early Church. The Apostles' Creed was my lifeline. For years it served as my de facto creed. In more recent years, the Old Roman Symbol—the forerunner to the Apostles' Creed—has supplanted it. But even then, all my beliefs can easily be summed up in Jesus' simple statement: "Love Your Neighbor."[1]

I have come to believe that anyone who requires anything beyond "Love God/Love Others" to follow Jesus is probably going too far, in my opinion. Work out your own salvation, yes, but don't try to work out the salvation of others.[2]

In my early years, I used an ever-shifting rubric to determine the validity or veracity of a person's faith. But now, if someone tells me they are a Christian, I believe them. And if I ever have questions about a person's true allegiance to Christ, I don't look to their beliefs as much as I look to their fruit, their levels of love, joy, peace, forbearance, kindness, goodness, faithfulness, gentleness, and self-control.[3]

Like Jesus said, you will know who my true followers are by the way they love each other, and you'll know those that don't truly follow me because of their lack of love for each other.[4]

As I reconstructed a healthier set of core beliefs, I learned that what I *don't* believe is often more important than what I *do* believe. Secondary things should remain secondary. Noncreedal beliefs are necessarily noncreedal, and those who attempt to ignore, avoid, or rewrite the creeds to make the enclosure around Christianity smaller probably do not have my or God's best interests in mind.

---

[1] Mark 12:30–31.

[2] Philippians 2:12.

[3] Galatians 5:22–23.

[4] John 13:35.

What makes a great creed isn't what's baked into it; it's what is left out.

And by the way, if anyone from my fundamentalist church roots happens to get this far in the book: first, RESPECT! Thanks for being so willing to listen. Second, "No Creed but Christ" is technically a creed.

Reflect

1. What song best sums up what you believe about life?
2. What is something that used to be a core belief in your life, but no longer is?
3. What is your opinion on the usefulness/helpfulness of creeds?
4. Name one of your first-tier (core) beliefs and one of your second-tier (less important) beliefs.
5. Write a personal creed of at least five lines, defining the most important core beliefs you hold to be true.

13 Pilgrimage

Not all those who wander are lost.

—J.R.R. Tolkien

It is 2:00 a.m. and my alarm is again playing a pleasant sound at this most unpleasant hour. Though my simple room and the world beyond it are quite dark, it is my final morning at the Abbey and my heart is finally filled with a bit of light and hope.

Perhaps this journey to the Abbey was worth my time after all.

My ears register a familiar sound from beyond the warmth and safety of my window. *Rain.* Its very presence threatens to wash away the meager light that has taken hold in my heart.

Pants? … check …

Boots? … check …

Umbrella? … check …

Headlamp? … check …

I enter the night.

It isn't until the Retreat House is long behind me that I realize the torch to which I have entrusted my journey is woefully inadequate for the job. It struggles to pierce the darkness *and* the driving rain. It wages a war that the night seems intent on winning.

The now well-worn path through the fields between the Retreat House and the Abbey eventually wanders through a beautiful pine grove before breaking into an enormous clearing at the foot of the cross that has been so central to my time at the Abbey.

My little headlamp notwithstanding, the path is difficult to traverse at night, but the fog of my breath, the glare of the lamp, and the blistering rain all conspire against me to make it even worse. It is as though some force is concerned about the flickering light within, hoping to snuff it out before it grows into a raging bonfire.

Despite the difficulty of the going, I find my heart strangely more in tune with words of prayer than night-time navigation. These prayers from within the throes of darkness wander along to my wife and children. I pray that they are warm and asleep, resting in the sweet calm of Christ—unlike myself at this present hour. I find an odd sense of comfort and peace in the opportunity to pray for them as I wage war against the darkness—praying for them at a time when they cannot pray for themselves. This spirit of prayer on the journey helps my soul to hold on to a bit of the light it has found this week. Try as it may, I will not let the darkness destroy my flicker of life.

Fully alone—and now in the middle of nowhere—I have left the warm light of the Retreat House behind but am not yet able to see the light of the Abbey ahead. It is here, in this place of total solitude, that one of the most terrifying experiences of my life was about to occur.

Unless you have ever been in the middle of nowhere, alone, without self-defense tools or a way to call for help, you cannot fully comprehend the sheer terror of seeing two large eyes, your height, but not human, reflected back to you in the darkness.

I am *not* alone.

I immediately know what they are. Eyes. But I have no idea to whom—or worse, *what*—they belong. Adrenaline courses through my body. Sheer terror grips my heart.

Friend or foe?

Fight or flight?

I realize that while there are many animals that prefer darkness to light, there are relatively few that I would mind meeting up close and personal.

Just as I am about to turn and run—and probably shriek the most embarrassing scream of all time—the animal comes into focus, moving from the shadowlands of fear into the faltering light of my mind and heart.

A deer!

Sigh.

Motionless, the deer stands atop the crest of a hill at the edge of the pine grove. It is looking directly at me, yet not just *at* me but *into* me. There is an overwhelming feeling that this animal is staring directly and deeply into my soul, a feeling that I had never felt up until that moment and haven't since.

I pause for a second time, unable to move.

I am a prisoner to this other-worldly stare.

And there, much like it had at the beginning of the week, my soul began to unravel at its seams. But this time, it unwound years of hidden heartache and sorrow as it spun out. The rain was no match for my tears as the emotions poured like a rushing torrent. Memories of the past, pain from the present, and fears about the future ripped their way out of the deep recesses of my soul and spilled themselves all over my face.

A verse from the songs within Psalms forced its way to the front of my mind:

As the deer longs for streams of water,
so I long for you, O God.[1]

Here was God saying it to me once again: *I am here; I see you.*

It was there, on the final journey from Bethlehem Retreat House to the Abbey, that I finally found certainty that God was holding more than the world in his hands.

... God was holding me.

As I crested the hill that breaks into the clearing at the foot of the cross just before the Abbey, it all finally began to make sense. The House Mother at Bethlehem had said that the journey from the Retreat House to the Abbey is about .6 miles.

Why give such a precise number? I wondered. *Why not simply say a half mile?*

But now I get it.

The journey from Bethlehem House to the cross at the Abbey is a walk of about .6 miles; the journey from Bethlehem city to the Jerusalem cross of Christ is a walk of about 6 miles. And to me, in this moment, the Abbey and its cross feel very much like Jerusalem and its cross: the center of my hope and site of my redemption.

With the Abbey now clearly in view, I realize that somewhere between Bethlehem and Jerusalem the rain has stopped. I set my headlamp and umbrella aside, no longer needing them to protect me from the night or the surprises it might contain.

I am home.

---

[1]Psalm 42:1.

Like many words that come to us from the distant past, *pilgrimage* is built by way of butting two words against one another and allowing them to together create a new path forward. From the Latin word *pergrinus, pilgrimage* is built by uniting *per* (meaning "through") and *ager* (meaning "field" or "land"). The word is intentionally built to suggest a journey *through* something. Not just *to* a destination, but *through* it.

Sometimes well-meaning travelers—such as dads determined to get their families to a destination come hell or high water, or pastors who place the goals of the institution over the individuals in it—become too overly focused on the destination. The concept of pilgrimage, on the other hand, asks travelers to consider the value of the getting there.

Humans have been making pilgrimage journeys for as long as anyone can remember, and many people are brought up believing that pilgrimage is a necessary component of a well-lived life. Epic tales like Homer's *Odyssey,* Bunyan's *The Pilgrim's Progress,* Chaucer's *Canterbury Tales,* and Mark Twain's *Huckleberry Finn* encourage us to consider the power of an intentional pilgrimage.

Over the years, I have been surprised to find a number of important journeys in the Bible. Take Abram, for example, to whom "the Lord had said to Abram, 'Go …'"[2] Abram complies,

---

[2] Genesis 12:1a, NIV.

packing his belongings, gathering his family, and setting out. Oddly enough, God doesn't tell Abram where he is going before he sets out. God simply says, "... the land that I will show you."[3]

Consider that for a moment.

God initiates the action of Abram's journey without so much as a hint as to where the road will lead. It would seem that, sometimes, the destination isn't all that important.

Just one book later, an entire nation makes a pilgrimage of biblical proportions when the descendants of Abraham, Isaac, and Jacob make an exodus out of Egypt. Led by a cloud and tailed by the armies of Egypt, the Israelites become pilgrims in a harsh and strange land. Though their minds are set on reaching a promised land, God seems to think that their hearts needed a lengthy journey through a desert in order to be ready.

It was on the journey, *before* reaching the destination, that they (re)learn what it means to be people of God.

But perhaps the most poignant—and often fan favorite—biblical pilgrimage is recorded in the opening pages of the New Testament. There, the Apostle Matthew records how 400 years of God's silence were miraculously broken by the birth of Jesus. It is interesting that Matthew decides to avoid the riveting parts of the story that tell of a manger and shepherds, choosing to instead focus on the harrowing tale of a collection of magi who make a cross-continent pilgrimage to honor the birth of the King of the Jews.

Ever since these brave star-gazers brought their gifts, pilgrims have been wandering across land and sea with their souls set on heaven and their hearts longing for Jesus in the journey.

As important as pilgrimage was to their Jewish roots, the earliest Christians rarely practiced pilgrimage. There was little need. They lived in and around the primary sites related to the

[3] Genesis 12:1b.

birth of Christianity. But as Christianity began to spread, so did widespread persecution. Traveling Christians were easy targets, so Christians stayed home except to visit the tombs of local martyrs on the anniversary of their birth into Heaven.

It wasn't until Emperors Constantine and Licinius famously passed the Edict of Milan in 313 CE that extensive anti-Christian policies were abolished and people of faith were finally free to move about the empire as they wished.

Though centuries of oppression had limited religious travel among Christians, the stories of heroism among the martyrs of the faith had spread like wildfire. Now that Christians could freely travel, they were intent on visiting the cities and tombs of the courageous martyrs whose stories had been a source of strength and hope through the seemingly endless era of persecution. For many families, these trips to the tombs of the martyrs became annual pilgrimages as they hoped to never forget the heavy price paid during the years of terrible Roman persecution.

During the Middle Ages, pilgrimages experienced a second surge in popularity. Now, in addition to the tombs of martyrs and saints, Christians traveled to see holy relics and receive indulgences.

As can sometimes happen with acts of devotion, the practice of pilgrimage became counterproductive to faith. What had begun as a spiritual practice devoted to connecting with the intangible had become more about receiving something tangible.

Pilgrimage had lost its way.

For all of the negatives that the Reformation brought, its concern about the growing abuse of pilgrimage was not one of them. The reformers were right, but rather than reform it, the reformers rebuked it so strongly that the practice generally fell out favor until the modern era.

God's Presence through Pilgrimage

Of all the ancient spiritual practices of the Early Church, pilgrimage is by far the most popular. These ancient routes, once mostly abandoned, are now packed with pilgrims. Many new pilgrimage routes have emerged as a new generation of Christians find new destinations to visit that are meaningful to their faith, or to faith in the modern era.

Today, Christians are no longer alone in their understanding of the power inherent to spiritual pilgrimages. Many of today's pilgrims who travel ancient pilgrimage routes are not people of faith at all. Yet they travel these routes with a deep desire to devote themselves to *something*. Those who embark on pilgrimages today find what many in the Early Church found—there can be great spiritual value in the simple act of going for a walk. The attractiveness of intentional pilgrimage shouldn't surprise us, though. As the world grows more progressively connected, people increasingly feel the need to disconnect. Walking an ancient path allows us to disconnect from the present in order to reconnect to something bigger than ourselves.

Though many find faith, or strength, on pilgrim paths, not everyone is a believer. Reflecting on his childhood, theologian and Bishop of Durham N.T. Wright blames his reluctance to practice pilgrimage on his thoroughly Protestant upbringing, saying, "there was a strong sense, indeed, that place and buildings could actually get in the way" of God's presence and power.[4]

Wright has long since changed his mind, and perhaps, so should we.

The Reformers' primary concern with pilgrimage was not so much the *practice* of pilgrimage itself, but the *objects of devotion*

---

[4] N.T. Wright, *The Way of the Lord: Christian Pilgrimage Today* (Eerdmans, 1999), 2.

that drove self-centered and spiritually dubious pilgrimages. Saints, relics, tombs, churches, and other "holy" places had ceased to point people to *the* object of devotion—Jesus—and instead became objects of devotion themselves.

It was, in a manner of speaking, worshipping the created rather than the Creator. We should be careful to be too harsh on them, though. We tend to have the same difficulty.

Part of my growing disconnect with the streams of Evangelicalism in which I swam was the movement's worship of things other than Jesus. Bigger church buildings became objects of devotion. Church-related events, conferences, and activities became a higher priority than serving and loving our neighbors. The Bible became an untouchable spiritual object, the fourth member of the Trinity, vying with Jesus for prominence. Indulgences in the form of forgiveness were offered to miserable politicians who did the bidding of the Christian voter. Devotion to the faith was proven through attendance, tithing, and political voting rather than the Beatitudes.

Places, buildings, and political power are still getting in the way of God's presence, even today.

On the path at the Abbey, I began to wonder if recentering our faith on ancient paths and places might, today, reconnect us to something deeper than a modern faith lived in the shallows of 2,000 years of wisdom.

I instinctively knew that I did not need to visit Jerusalem or travel the Camino de Santiago to experience the presence of God. God comes to his people. But I wondered what might happen if I began making more intentional journeys.

Of course, no one needs to become a pilgrim to experience the presence of God, but how could I discount the overwhelming number of examples from the Old Testament, New Testament, and Early Church who *did* make journeys to holy places due to a desire to better experience the presence and power of

God? These ancient pilgrims learned what many other spiritual travelers throughout the ages have also discovered:

> *Leaving one's present location for a spiritual journey (a pilgrimage) creates unique opportunities for God to break through the mundane rhythms of everyday life that regularly burden and distract.*

This is exactly what I had done!

This was the reason I had come to the Abbey.

I doubt whether I would have ever experienced a reawakening or reconstruction of my faith had I never made a pilgrimage to a western New York Abbey.

The familiar often obscures the divine.

A pilgrimage forces a person to leave the familiar, opening themself to the eternal and transcendent. By setting one's *feet* toward something—God, for example—a person also sets their *mind* and *heart* more fully toward God.

My pilgrimage didn't bring God closer to me; it brought my heart closer to God.

Pilgrimage doesn't bring God closer to the pilgrim, but brings the heart of the pilgrim in closer proximity to God.

It is not the destination that matters as much as one's willingness to leave behind something lesser in order to move toward something greater. There can be great value in making an intentional journey, wherever it may be, if spiritual growth is the desired outcome.

And yet, the destination one chooses *is* of some importance. Without the motivation of somewhere to go, it is unlikely that many potential pilgrims would ever begin a journey at all!

On that point, agreement can be found with the ancients: true pilgrimage is not just travel to a place, but rather, travel to a place of profound significance.

Pilgrimage is a journey to a place that is *holy for the pilgrim*, a place where the membrane between this world and the reality beyond this world is especially thin, a place where a transcendent reality impinges on the immanent reality of the present. It may not necessarily be that the pilgrim's destination is itself a holy or "thin" space in and of itself, but that it is a location where the membrane between the person's *own* heart and the heart of God is especially thin.

By that definition, any location of personal meaning will do as a pilgrimage destination. The best pilgrimages are to places of great personal significance, places where we find safe spaces that resonate with our history, our soul, or our journey.

The best pilgrimages take us to "thin spaces" where we can contemplate where we are and where we are going in life.

Reconstructing Pilgrimage

In the years after the Abbey, I began to see that Jesus regularly used the road as an opportunity to teach important lessons about faith. In fact, most of the New Testament's gospel accounts take place on the road between one place and another. I began taking the long way rather than the shortcut on trips. If we passed a random farmer's market or county fair on the way to somewhere, I would pull over and enjoy it, sometimes with the whole family … sometimes alone.

This spiritual practice helped me to see that the best lessons in life come on the journey.

As a family, we began to identify and visit areas of significance to *our* story: a trip to the graves of old family saints in another state, a trip to old family homes, and trips to former places of worship became commonplace. Each of these journey-pilgrimages was an opportunity to tell our children the stories of our faith, point out Ebenezers, and pray for God to continue to move mightily in our family's future.

I committed to taking each of my four children on a traditional pilgrimage before they left the house for good. One has been completed—the Holy Land—and there are three more left to go: European Cathedrals with one child, Greece with another, and the one I am most looking forward to, the Camino de Santiago.

Personally, I committed to making pilgrimages to places that hold spiritual significance in my own life. To name a few: the old family cemeteries in Ricetown, Kentucky, and Connersville, Indiana; my grandparents' old Indiana homestead; the churches I have pastored over the years; Orcas Island; and the Starbucks Roastery in Seattle.

And, of course, the Abbey of the Genesee.

As the service in the Abbey came to a close somewhere around 3:30 a.m., my body longed to be back in bed and my mind began to wander.

Had the rain begun again?

Looking to my feet, I was thankful for the last-minute decision to pack a pair of hiking boots. They aren't much to look at anymore; any other person would have long since tossed them out. The boots are more than a decade old and are showing their age. Dirt, mud, and dust from many roads and ascents cling to the shoes. Though I've tried, the grime now seems to defy removal, so I leave it as a sign of my wanderlust … and of having given up. I am thankful for their companionship this night but wonder if this is our final journey together. It would be a fitting, though lackluster, end.

These boots and I have been up and down mountains together. They once helped me summit the fourth highest peak in the Continental 48. At some point over the years, these boots became more than shoes to me; they became friends. I hated to see them go, which is why I have hung on to them long past their prime.

The service into which they are now pressed is far lighter duty than that to which they had once been called. The gentle rise and fall of the Genesee's grassy paths could not compare to the glory of a 14,000-foot Colorado Rocky peak. These shoes had seen more exhilarating adventures than the Abbey, but I wondered if this journey was perhaps their most significant mission yet.

Could the journey of this week—this pilgrimage of the soul—be the most important journey on which they had ever, or would ever, carry me?

Could it be that their last full measure of devotion was to see mine renewed?

The bells chime, the service ends, and I bundle up to make my way one last time along the path from the Abbey to my bed of sleep. In a few hours I would be returning to life, somehow different … but how?

The clouds have broken!

As I pass the cross, I again note the lights of the cities down the valley and up the mountain beyond, and the seamless blanket of sparkling light that stretches from the foot of the cross into the heights of the heavens. It is a glorious display of the thin membrane between God and man that meets somewhere on the horizon.

The final psalm of the night's Vigil remains in my heart:

They almost finished me off,
but I refused to abandon your commandments.
In your unfailing love, spare my life;
then I can continue to obey your laws.[5]

Pondering these words in the darkness along the trail, I realize that the path that lies before me is now gloriously covered in a heavy frost. The cold, dark journey for which I had been deeply ungrateful not more than an hour ago had contained all the ingredients necessary to create this beauty. Without the harsh elements I had endured before—the ones that had made me utterly miserable—the majesty on display in the present would have never been.

Soaking in the beauty, I looked down at just the right moment to see footsteps imprinted into the frost-laden path. Concern crept at the edge of my heart.

Was someone else on the path in front of me?

Pointing my torch down the trail revealed nothing more than a fine blanket of frost stretching in all ways beyond the length of my vision.

I stood staring for far too long at the footprints, captivated by them.

There was something strangely familiar about these footfalls, the impression was not unlike my old hiking boots.

Wait!

These *were* my footprints, made not more than an hour ago as I made my pilgrimage through darkness and fear.

These impressions were the only remnants of the journey and the only true evidence that I had indeed walked this way to

[5] Psalm 119:87–88.

keep vigil in darkness under the light of the Abbey. For whatever reason, the frost of the night had been unable to overtake the impressions made by my having passed this way.

The cold, dark night had *tried* to hide the evidence of my journey but had ultimately failed to erase my steps of faith.

I wondered … hoped … that this was another message from God.

I longed to know that my life had indeed made a difference and that the effects of my efforts would not be completely erased even though, for a while, they may lie unseen.

I *had* made an impression. I was sure of it!

Try as the oppressive dark night I had endured might try, something of my journey of faith would last.

And then, it hit me square between the eyes.

These five visible footfalls lay in the very spot where, just an hour ago, I had encountered the deer that looked so deeply into my soul.

As God is my witness:

The.
Exact.
Same.
Spot.

Though many events and lessons in my pilgrimage to the Abbey were as of yet unclear, it was now fully transparent to me that God was with me on this journey.

Immanuel: God with *me*.

Pondering these things in amazement, I exited the pine grove into the expanse of field between the Abbey and Bethlehem, and my heart skipped a beat at what lay before me.

The miles of open fields—now fully covered in deep frost and sitting calmly beneath the clear light of a full moon—were shimmering in a glorious display of dazzling light. I was nearly blinded in the dead of night by the brilliant display. Beams of reflected moonlight were streaking across the ground and sky in the most wonderful show that I have ever seen. The ground looked as though it were covered in a blanket of billions of diamonds, shimmering like stars for as far as my eyes could see in all directions.

I could barely breathe, the glory of it all arresting my very soul in a moment of awe and wonder. I imagined that it must be like the Apostle John's experience when he was caught up into heaven on the Isle of Patmos.

And in that moment, on that path, I was not completely sure that I *wasn't* in heaven.

And wherever the path of my life led from here, I was certain that God would be with me on it.

Even be it only us.

Reflect

1. Can you think of a movie, book, or song that is about pilgrimage?
2. Is there a particular place where you always feel closer to the divine?
3. Have you ever made a pilgrimage of any sort? If so, where did you go and what was your experience?
4. If you had the resources (time, money, freedom, health) to make a pilgrimage to anywhere in the world, and knew (no matter how difficult) that you would be successful, where would you go?
5. If you were to go on a pilgrimage, is there a particular question that you would be seeking an answer?
6. List the five places most important to making you who you currently are. How often do you visit them, and what happens when you do?

14 Wreckage and Mess

> Let all guests who arrive be received like Christ, for He is going to say, "I came as a guest, and you received Me." (Matthew 25:35)
>
> —St. Benedict of Nursia

My meager accommodations in Bethlehem now looked like they had when I arrived: empty and awaiting a new pilgrim. My bag was packed, my bed made, and a silent goodbye had been offered to the House Mother.

I might even admit to having shed a tear or two.

The time had finally come to leave the safety of the Abbey and make my way home … toward what I was now certain would also be a new life. I was still a mess, sure, but somehow, against all hope, I had begun to reconstruct my faith from the wreckage of what had been.

I didn't know how all of the pieces would fit back together, exactly which pieces I needed to let go of, or even what the picture would look like in the end, but I was confident that I had everything I needed to move forward.

The Abbey had given me everything I had needed to find the ancient path of The Way.

All that was left to do was to take in a final hour of prayer.

It was 6:00 a.m. and the bright light of a new dawn was pushing the darkness behind the horizon. I found myself face-to-face one final time with the doors of the Abbey.

The entryway that had once been my archnemesis had now become friend and savior. It no longer seemed as imposing or impenetrable to me as it once had.

Perhaps I looked different to it as well.

I *felt* different.

Was I … different?

I had arrived at the Abbey with more questions than answers. Questions like *Who am I?*, *Why am I here?*, and *How did I get here?* had haunted me. Now, I was leaving with more answers than questions.

The road ahead would not be easy, but I was absolutely certain that I finally had the strength to walk the road forward, wherever it may lead.

The hour of Lauds is traditionally the most important of all the hours of prayer. It is celebrated at daybreak, when the sun is dispelling the night and a new day is being born. The church has always considered the sun to be a symbol of Christ rising from the dead.

This hour of prayer during the first light of day is an opportunity to express joy and optimism. It is also the only service of the day in which the Abbey offers the Eucharist. As a Protestant in a Catholic monastery, communion is closed to me, but a Blessing is not.

I am barely able to pay attention as the service progresses; I can hardly wait to finally receive my Blessing from the priest …

my first and only of the week. It would be the perfect way to end the pilgrimage that changed the course of my life.

When it is time for my row to make its way to the front, I stand up and step out of my comfort zone. We wend our way toward the priest, who cuts a rather striking and angelic figure in a brilliant white outfit trimmed in gold.

When it is my turn, I cross my arms at the chest to indicate that I am not Catholic, and as such, am an outsider hoping to receive a Blessing instead. I will be the only person to do this act, and I feel awkward and exposed. I sheepishly make eye contact with him, gird up my emotions, and step forward.

There is a long uncomfortable pause as a look of surprise crosses the priest's face, and he simply stares at me for what feels like an eternity. The pause is so long, in fact, that I nearly just turn and leave. But just before I am about to rush away from the moment, his surprise is washed away by a warm smile that seemed to hold an ocean of love.

Father John, the officiating priest, had seen me in regular attendance at every other hour of prayer over the last week. He had surely noticed me, the sole attendee at each nightly 2:00 a.m. Vigil. And I now realized that Father John had erroneously judged me to be the most committed of Catholics. He had, until now, been blissfully unaware that I had arrived, not the most committed of Catholics, but the most broken of Protestants.

He stretched out his arms, bringing the body of Christ to his lips. Through it, he spoke with a booming confidence that resonated through the Abbey louder than any spoken word I had experienced that week. His voice carried the force that I suspect Moses experienced on the mountain or the crowd at Jesus' baptism as God spoke. And I believe that Father John intended just that type of moment, the voice of God channeled directly to the Kevin of the past, the Kevin of the present, and the Kevin of the future.

His voice echoed for an eternity, and through eternity, I am certain:

BLESS YOU, my son.

It was, to me, as if the words had come from the very lips of Christ himself, and I believe that they had.

Yes … Bless me.

It was time to bid goodbye to the Abbey, and in my leaving, begin to put into practice the lessons that I had learned. As I forced myself to turn and leave the Abbey for the last time, I ran into Father John again. The very same Father John who—not more than an hour before—had presided over my final prayer service and first Eucharist at the Abbey.

He was now making his way into the restroom.

Father John had traded in his angelic robes for much simpler attire—gray overalls and work boots. The hands that had once held the chalice and wafer were now holding a bucket and scrub brush.

He looked at me and chuckled.

"Humble work," he said.

He had guessed what I was thinking.

"The last monk who cleaned the restrooms was over a hundred years old, but he died a few years ago and now it's my duty. He used to walk around the Abbey waving pieces of toilet paper after scrubbing the toilets. 'We're not angels yet,'" he would say. "'We're not angels yet.' And then he'd go back to cleaning."

No, I thought, *we're not.*

And then I chuckled.

The monks had taught me many lessons that week, but perhaps this was the most important one.

Jesus certainly meets us in communion and on ancient paths, yes.

But also,

There is no mess in which Jesus will not meet us.

There is no wreckage from which he cannot redeem us.

Epilogue

"I walked away."

Here I was again, hearing the same gut-punch ending to a story that I had grown weary of hearing. This was the eighth time. Or was it the ninth? I had lost count.

I was a pastor, but these weren't congregants. These were friends. Old friends. Good friends. The kind that remain friends even after years of little or no contact.

Wait, no, I wasn't a pastor.

Even a month after resigning, it was tough to reframe my identity.

Four weeks earlier, I had drawn a line in the sand between myself and toxic institutional churches, saying, "No more."

Walking away was one of the hardest and easiest things I have ever done. Hard to admit that I couldn't fix what is broken in the church. Easy to end the nonstop cycle of ongoing church hurt.

"I've heard that story before," I told my friend on the other end of the phone call. And I had, eight (or nine) other times.

They had been committed followers of Christ, spiritually mature, actively involved in the church, and giants of faith.

At least, I thought they were, until every single one of them shocked me by outing themselves as ex-Evangelical, ex-church, and for a couple, ex-Christian.

None of them had left the church or their faith willfully. They felt they had no choice.

None of them had felt comfortable telling me. I was a part of the structures that had ultimately failed them.

None of them had lost their faith, though.

They could not see what I could see. The light of Christ, though nearly extinguished by their church trauma, was still lit in their soul.

They had not walked away from Christ; the church had walked away from them.

I understood.

I, too, had walked away from the institutional church.

But here, in them and their abandonment, I found a greater pastoral need. I found the church outside the church. I walked toward:

- Christ.
- Truth and integrity.
- My family's spiritual health.
- Those who have been hurt by the church too.
- The abused, abandoned, ostracized, and outright ignored.
- Those who were disappointed, disillusioned, and done.
- Those who wanted to be close to Christ and feel his life … but could no longer walk into a church.

For the first time since my experience at the Abbey almost a decade before, I felt relief. I even felt a renewed sense of hope for the institutional church. Perhaps things *could* be different.

I had found my mission.

I had found my voice.

I began meeting people online and around tables, re-creating the warmth, hospitality, and practices that had embedded themselves in me years before. Each week, we would invite weary pilgrims from church wars to simply lay down their burdens and rest. We met them where they were, and let them stay and heal, no strings attached.

Today, I get to:

- Speak freely, rattle cages, and flip the occasional table.
- Preach the true gospel in all of its weird and radical glory.
- Equip people to grow in their faith and fellowship with God.
- Push back against syncretism and Christian Nationalism.
- Help people see what the Bible truly does and doesn't teach.
- Fight for the oppressed.
- Minister to a ragtag bunch of incredible saints.
- Re-implement Early Church wisdom.
- Challenge the institutional church.
- Use my privilege to tear down strongholds built and defended by other privileged people.
- Wake up and do what I love.

My faith is stronger than it has ever been … all because I threw up my hands at the mess that was the institutionalized church and said:

Here am I, Lord. Send me?
Wherever you lead, I will follow.

Index

F

G